PENGUIN BOOKS

A YEAR WITH HAFIZ

HAFIZ, whose given name was Shams-ud-din Muhammad (c. 1320–1389), is the most beloved poet of Persians. He was born and lived in Shiraz, a beautiful garden city, where he became a famous spiritual teacher. His *Divan* (collected poems) is a classic in the literature of Sufism and mystical verse. The work of Hafiz became known to the West largely through the passion of Goethe. His enthusiasm deeply affected Ralph Waldo Emerson, who then translated Hafiz in the nineteenth century. Emerson said, "Hafiz is a poet for poets," and Goethe remarked, "Hafiz has no peer." Hafiz's poems were also admired by such diverse notables as Nietzsche and Arthur Conan Doyle, whose wonderful character Sherlock Holmes quotes Hafiz; García Lorca praised him; the famous composer Johannes Brahms was so touched by his verse he put several lines into compositions; and even Queen Victoria was said to have consulted the works of Hafiz in times of need. The range of Hafiz's verse is indeed stunning. He says, "I am a hole in a flute that the Christ's breath moves through—listen to this music." In another poem Hafiz playfully sings, "Look at the smile on the earth's lips this morning, she lay again with me last night."

DANIEL LADINSKY is one of the most successful living writers in the world working with poetry. His work has reached millions of people. Daniel lived in India for six years, where he worked in a rural clinic free to the poor, and was a student of the essence and unity of all faiths. A teacher there ingrained the wonder of Hafiz into his soul when he said, "With great wit and tenderness the words of Hafiz speak for God." Ladinsky's other books include *The Gift, Love Poems from God, The Subject Tonight Is Love, I Heard God Laughing,* and an upcoming Rumi book, *The Purity of Desire.* Once, when Daniel was asked a reason for his accomplishments and if he had any advice for other artists, Daniel quoted a line from an old Broadway musical that went, "You gotta have heart, miles and miles and miles of heart!"

A YEAR WITH

Hafiz

DAILY
CONTEMPLATIONS

DANIEL LADINSKY

PENGUIN BOOKS

Penguin Books
Published by the Penguin Group
Penguin Group (USA) Inc., 375 Hudson Street, New York, New York 10014, U.S.A.
Penguin Group (Canada), 90 Eglinton Avenue East, Suite 700, Toronto, Ontario, Canada M4P 2Y3
(a division of Pearson Penguin Canada Inc.)
Penguin Books Ltd, 80 Strand, London WC2R 0RL, England
Penguin Ireland, 25 St Stephen's Green, Dublin 2, Ireland (a division of Penguin Books Ltd)
Penguin Group (Australia), 250 Camberwell Road, Camberwell, Victoria 3124, Australia
(a division of Pearson Australia Group Pty Ltd)
Penguin Books India Pvt Ltd, 11 Community Centre, Panchsheel Park, New Delhi - 110 017, India
Penguin Group (NZ), 67 Apollo Drive, Rosedale, Auckland 0632, New Zealand
(a division of Pearson New Zealand Ltd)
Penguin Books (South Africa) (Pty) Ltd, 24 Sturdee Avenue, Rosebank, Johannesburg 2196, South Africa

Penguin Books Ltd, Registered Offices:
80 Strand, London WC2R 0RL, England

First published in Penguin Books 2011

7   9   10   8

Copyright © Daniel Ladinsky, 2011
All rights reserved

Some of the selections first appeared in the following books by Daniel Ladinsky, published by Penguin
Books: *The Gift: Poems of Hafiz; I Heard God Laughing: Poems of Hope and Joy, Renderings of Hafiz; Love
Poems from God: Twelve Sacred Voices from the East and West;* and *The Subject Tonight is Love: 60 Wild and
Sweet Poems of Hafiz.* Copyright © Daniel Ladinsky, 1996, 1999, 2002, 2006.

"The Life and Work of Hafiz" by Henry S. Mindlin from *I Heard God Laughing: Renderings of Hafiz* by
Daniel Ladinsky (Sufism Reoriented, 1996). By permission of Sufism Reoriented.

LIBRARY OF CONGRESS CATALOGING-IN-PUBLICATION DATA
Hafiz, 14th cent.
[Poems. English. Selections.]
A year with Hafiz : daily contemplations / Daniel Ladinsky.
p.   cm.
Includes bibliographical references.
ISBN 978-0-14-311754-4
1. Hafiz, 14th cent.—Translations into English.   2. Sufi poetry, Persian—Translations into English.
I. Ladinsky, Daniel James.   II. Title.
PK6465.Z31L344 2010
891'.5511—dc22
2009052982

Printed in the United States of America
Set in Adobe Garamond Pro

ALWAYS LEARNING   PEARSON

It rises,
a glorious sun,
if one can sit quiet long enough.
Seeing it, one feels, I now have everything,
everything I could
ever want.

* * *

There
are moments
in moist love when heaven
is jealous of what
we on earth
can do.

—HAFIZ

God has treasuries beneath the Throne,
the keys to which are the tongues of poets.

—HADITH OF THE PROPHET MUHAMMAD

ACKNOWLEDGMENTS

I thank my teacher, Eruch Jessawala, with whom I spent a lot of time over a twenty-year period. I think he knew Hafiz intrinsically, more truly and deeply than anyone I have ever met. Not one poem of mine would ever have been published without his extraordinary sanction and a profound, rare insight he revealed to me about my work. And I thank his decades-old little bamboo walking stick—*that Zen's master's baton*—that I *journeyed* next to for hundreds of miles in India. It lays across my computer as I write. I think my every word leans against it and upon Eruch, in many ways. For he is now the hub of me, and I a spoke he moves.

Nancy Barton, an old friend and now my agent, made a fantastic contribution to this book in many ways. Carolyn Carlson, my wonderful editor of nearly a decade . . . hey, looks like we finally got this out—a glass click and big smooch.

CONTENTS

RALPH WALDO EMERSON,
A PSYCHIATRIST I KNOW,
AND MY PORTRAIT OF HAFIZ

They took a little walk on the wild side, they even got a bit outrageous, some of these Hafiz renderings. Their wings could not resist unfurling, breaking out of conventional space and cultural-bound time, hoping to lift many in the wake of their freedom. How did that ever happen? Well, truth is—the gods probably had all these poems up their sleeves way before I was born. My bucket just drew them from a well. And I think Hafiz would stand behind my artistic license with his work, moreover encourage it, as I feel so much of the *original* has been lost. And whatever can make us more sane and *organic*, perhaps aid in discerning the real, I feel a duty to offer. No holds barred, to me, is rule number one in poetry, and in all true art or service that cares only to comfort and inspire. An at times *healthy lawlessness*, can be just that, something a wise angel prescribes. Which to my mind translates into verses like—Moses and the Pinup Girl and Spiritual La-La Land ... making a debut. Some wanted me to take Moses and his sweetheart out of this book. But hell, Hafiz only cared about love. And I feel he gave my pen a wink.

Helpful I hope these poems are, and there is seriousness here. I have wept over many of these poems as they explored theological heights and mixed with our heart's beautiful, everyday emotions. The common is applauded and revealed as sacred. There is wonderful wit in some lines. The playful is turned loose and so is intelligence. The hallmark of Hafiz is to create a bond with his reader, and then offer his hand, when one might most need it. Hafiz was a true master in every sense of the word. A dear friend to any in spiritual need. Only the remarkable can do justice to him. I feel one has to take great liberties, at times, from some prevailing scholarly views of Hafiz to accomplish that; one's work then becomes controversial and vulnerable to criticism. What to do? So-called scholarship in regards to Hafiz can, it seems to me, greatly compromise his spirit and make him appear far less than I have seen and know he is.

Some have suggested I call my poems "Hafiz inspired" rather than "versions" or "renderings." That word *inspired* has always seemed a *step up*, if you will, for it in part means "breathed into by the divine." Well, all that seems so intimate and private, but maybe that is exactly what happened, and now I am just trying to exhale light—some gods or God, the soul of Hafiz—onto the page the best I can.

RALPH & TECHNICAL INFO

Most of the poems in this book have not been published before. Included here are the first of my renderings based on the translations of Hafiz by Ralph Waldo Emerson. It was British orientalist, Sir William Jones (1746–1794), who first pioneered English translations of Hafiz and other notable Persian poets into European literary culture. It was Emerson though, who offered the earliest translations of Hafiz to the world via an American pen. Emerson's Hafiz translations appear to have been made entirely from German sources. They were primarily created working from a collection of Hafiz's poems that was published in 1812 by Joseph von Hammer-Purgstall. Hammer-Purgstall's work had inspired Goethe to translate Hafiz in his famous *West-östlicher Divan*. Emerson read Goethe's versions and was deeply moved by them. Emerson was also an earnest student of a wide variety of books of Eastern philosophy, religion, history, and poetry. In the spring of 1846, Emerson purchased Hammer-Purgstall's Hafiz translations from the bookstore of his friend, Elizabeth Peabody. She was a colleague of his in the Transcendentalist movement. In subsequent years Hafiz became a life-long companion to Emerson and deeply influenced his remaining literary career. Emerson's journals clearly testify to this. Hafiz was apparently the person-ification of a human being and poet to him. For Emerson wrote, "He fears nothing. He sees too far, he sees throughout; such is the only man I wish to see or be." And Emerson gave Hafiz that wonderful, famous compliment when he said, "Hafiz is a poet for poets."

In many of the poems Emerson translated, he appears to have clearly collaborated upon, expanded, and even re-created Hafiz's verse. Of this sort of top-end literary tampering, Sir William Jones, who was considered a linguistic genius, said of *his own* paraphrased translations, in his *A Grammar of the Persian Language* (W. and J. Richardson, London, 1771), "When the learner is able to understand the images and allusions in the Persian poems, he will see a reason in every line why they cannot be translated literally into any European language."

Some extraordinary, thorough scholarship has been done regard-ing Emerson's Hafiz work. The most impressive I have come across is *The Topical Notebooks of Ralph Waldo Emerson,* Volume 2, edited by Ronald A. Bosco, with the chief editor being Ralph H. Orth (University of Missouri Press, 1993). Also, the book titled *Emerson: Collected Poems & Translations* published by the Library of America (1994) is another wonderful source of Emerson's work with Hafiz and other Persian and historic poets. According to these two sources, Emerson worked on more than one hundred poems of Hafiz, with several of those poems appearing incomplete, or *still in progress.* I hope I have added to that *progress.*

Emerson passed away on April 27, 1882. In honor of Emerson's remarkable endorsement—imprimatur—of Hafiz, I have devoted the entire month of April to Emerson's translations. I freely collaborated on Emerson's Hafiz poems, often trying to complete fragments of translations he left. Thus the poems in April are Hafiz-Hammer-Em-erson-Ladinsky poems. Wow, what a unique lineage, but perhaps the best one can do at the moment to continue to bring rightful attention to one of the priceless literary and spiritual treasures of the world.

A Psychiatrist I Know

I have a friend who is a practicing psychiatrist and she was an admirer of my work before we ever met. Of all the people I have spent time with, she is the deepest into Buddhist meditation and yoga. And at my request she sent me a month's worth of my Hafiz poems for this book. Her selections, she felt, most spoke to and could aid the intelligent heart, mind, and soul. Those selections, "from her professional understanding," could most benefit the psychological and spiritual *needs* of some of the thousands who each day visit professionals like herself, especially around the holidays. An interesting sanction, to my mind, of the poems she picked, and her involvement, was this: That literally within five minutes of my first asking her to contribute to this book . . . she sent me some 30 poems by email. I of course asked her how she could have possibly gotten those poems back to me so quickly and with so much apparent thought and insight. She replied, "I knew you were going to ask me to send those, so here they are." She had just returned from a whole week of intensive meditation in the mountains; maybe she got zapped by a satori or two and had a new radar system installed. Maybe we should go to her for treatment, or at least start meditating more. Her selections comprise the entries offered in November. In case things get especially rough over the holidays—or on any days—dip your cup in that Thanksgiving month, a *spiked punch bowl* served by a doctor who might cruise around in the Buddha's belly.

My Portrait of Hafiz

Besides the significant essay that follows this preface, "Releasing the Spirit of Hafiz" (first published in 1996), I would suggest that any who might be interested in more of the background and foundation of my working with Hafiz read "My Portrait of Hafiz"—via a reader's review I posted on Amazon.com for my book, *The Gift*. You should be able to easily find the review by simply *googling* "My Portrait of Hafiz," and following that a bit. That review essay is dated April 18, 2005. Also, I feel if Carl Jung were alive and I could have told him two astounding dreams/visions I have had of Hafiz in regards to my work, I bet Carl would have written a marvelous blurb.

A great thanks to any who support my work. My life has become these poems and books. May something in them touch you as only a real lover and friend can.

—DANIEL LADINSKY
JULY 10, 2011

P.S. A category-three *Marital Warning* (if it is not too late) from Rudyard Kipling, via some playful Hafiz sentiment that Kipling published in 1886 as "Certain Maxims of Hafiz" (this is maxim XI):

> *Pleasant the snaffle of courtship, improving the manners and carriage; but the colt (or filly*) who is wise will abstain from the terrible thorn-bit of marriage.*

---

* I added the word *filly* in there; seems I just can't stop tampering with things as they are. And *snaffle* means *a jointed bit, a bridle.*

RELEASING THE SPIRIT OF HAFIZ

My work with Hafiz began on an early morning walk in the countryside of central India, on a beautiful tree-lined road that leads to a place called Meherazad. This small, private residential community near the city of Ahmednagar was the home of the great spiritual Master, Avatar Meher Baba, until his passing in 1969. A small group of the Master's lifelong companions continue to live and work there, surrounded by a remarkable atmosphere of love.

I was walking with a man whom I have come to know as a teacher, a brother and a friend, a man who had been a member of the Master's circle since the late 1930s. On this particular morning, we were discussing Hafiz, who was Meher Baba's favorite poet. Though Hafiz lived in the fourteenth century, his verses are still immensely popular throughout the Near East and India. His insight and compassion, his subtle, expressive language and his deep reverence for beauty in all its forms have made him a favorite poet of lovers, and especially of lovers of God. The Sufis say that Hafiz loved so fully and so well that he became the living embodiment of Love. Meher Baba called him "a Perfect Master and a perfect poet."

Poetry was in the air at Meherazad that week. The day before our walk, we had listened to a program of marvelous English translations of Rumi, another Persian master poet, who lived a century before Hafiz. Now, as we walked, I turned to my mentor and companion and candidly said, "Compared to those splendid versions of Rumi we heard yesterday, the poetry of Hafiz can appear so pale in English! How can this be, when Meher Baba says that Hafiz is such a great poet?" He replied, "Baba has said it is because no one has yet properly translated Hafiz!" As soon as he said that, I was surprised to hear myself say, "I can do that!" That night, though I did not (and do not) know the Persian language, I wrote my first version of a Hafiz poem, working from a literal English translation.

For hundreds of years, people have struggled to find ways to reflect in English the sweetness and profundity of Hafiz's poetry. Some translators have tried to reproduce the rhythm, meter and rhyme of the original Persian, often bending and twisting English into strange and unfamiliar configurations to do so. Such careful efforts to honor the *form* of the poetry can sometimes ignore or violate the *spirit* of Hafiz—a spirit of infinite tenderness and compassion, of great exuberance, joy and laughter, of ecstatic love and fervent longing for his Beloved, and of wonder and delight at the divine splendor of the universe. I wanted to find ways to release that spirit in our own language.

The poems of Hafiz are mostly short love songs called *ghazals*, each one about the length of a sonnet. Scholars disagree about the exact number of poems that can be authenticated, but there are no more than eight hundred. Compared to Rumi and others, this is a tiny body of work. However, Hafiz created his poetry in a way that permits many kinds of interpretation. Persian is a flexible and mutable language, and Hafiz was an absolute master of it. Persian-speaking friends say that in some of his poems each word can have seven or eight shades of meaning and a variety of interpretations. A single couplet can be translated many different ways, and each one would be "right."

I quickly discovered that even in English, a single Hafiz poem, often a single couplet, could be approached from many points of view. A single stanza of Hafiz could generate whole families of independent poems in English, each exploring some aspect of the original. One might call the results "renderings" or renditions of Hafiz, rather than "translations." To "render" an artistic work means to interpret, to express, to realize. The word can also mean "surrendering" and "yielding"—in this case, opening to the guidance of the spirit contained within the poetry. Thus my poems are not "translations" in any traditional sense. They are not intended to be literal or scholarly or even "accurate." But I hope they are True—faithful to the living spirit of this divine poet.

These "renderings" are based on a remarkable translation of Hafiz by H. Wilberforce Clarke, originally published in 1891. I work from a beautiful two-volume, 1011-page edition of Clarke's work, recently republished in Iran. I also borrow and shape ideas and thoughts from a few of the many other available translations of Hafiz. A Select Bibliography of sources is included at the end of this book along with information about the life of Hafiz and the background of his poetry.

It is my understanding that when Hafiz created his poems, he often spoke them or sang them spontaneously and his companions wrote the verses down later. Even if one does not know Persian, it is easy to appreciate the rhythm and music of his "playful verse" when one hears it recited aloud. Many of his poems were set to popular tunes, and they are still sung now, six hundred years later, all over the East. Several of these English renderings have already inspired new songs of Hafiz for the West by many gifted musicians. I'm sure Hafiz would be delighted. These poems are meant to be recited, sung, even happily shouted—if it won't disturb the neighbors too much!

What can I say to my dear Master, Meher Baba, for all his help and guidance? Whatever truth, beauty, laughter and charm you may find here, I would say is a gift from him, the Avatar.

May these poems inspire us to give the great gift of kindness—to ourselves and to others.

—DANIEL LADINSKY
FEBRUARY 25, 1996

THE LIFE AND WORK OF HAFIZ

HENRY S. MINDLIN

Despite the popularity of Hafiz in the East, reliable information about the details of his life is sketchy. Scholars do not even agree about his dates of birth and death. He was probably born about 1320 and died about 1389, roughly the same dates as the first great poet who wrote in English, Geoffrey Chaucer. His given name was Shams-ud-din Muhammad. He chose the name Hafiz ("memorizer") as a pen name when he began to write poetry; it is a title given to someone who knows the entire Quran by heart, as he apparently did. Hafiz was born in Shiraz, a beautiful city in southern Persia that escaped the ravages of the Mongol and Tartar invasions during this violent and chaotic period of history. He spent nearly all of his life in this cultured garden city.

EARLY LIFE

All is written within the mind
To help and instruct the dervish
In dance and romance and prayer.

Hafiz did not have an easy or comfortable life. He was the youngest of three sons of poor parents. His father was a coal merchant who died when Hafiz was in his teens. To help support the family, Hafiz worked as a baker's assistant by day and put himself through school at night, using part of his salary to pay his tuition. Over many years, he mastered the subjects of a "classical" medieval education: Quranic law and theology, grammar, mathematics, and astronomy. He also mastered calligraphy, which in the centuries before printing was a highly refined art form. Islamic calligraphy was originally developed as a sacred art to preserve and glorify the Quran, the message of God. Since representational art was forbidden by religious law, calligraphy reached a remarkable degree of subtlety and expressiveness. Hafiz was a skilled draftsman and occasionally worked as a professional copyist.

His early education naturally included the great Persian poets: Saadi of Shiraz, Farid-ud-din Attar, Jalal-ud-din Rumi, and others. Poetry is a national art in Persia, somewhat like opera in Italy. Even in modern Iran, people at every social level know the great poets, argue passionately about their favorites, and quote them constantly in everyday conversation. In medieval Persia, the art of poetry was taken seriously and valued highly. Local princes and provincial governors employed court poets to create epic verses celebrating their greatness. When the ruler was especially pleased by a composition, the poet was sometimes placed on a scale and rewarded with his weight in gold.

A POET

A poet is someone
Who can pour light into a cup,
Then raise it to nourish
Your beautiful parched, holy mouth.

Hafiz had a natural poetic gift. Even as a child, he was able to improvise poems on any subject in any form and style. When he was in his early twenties, some of his love poems began to circulate in Shiraz, and he was soon invited to participate in poetry gatherings at court. He won the patronage of a succession of rulers and wealthy noblemen. One of his benefactors founded a religious college and offered

Hafiz a position a teacher. Thus, during his middle years, he served as a court poet and a college professor. He married and had at least one son.

Hafiz's livelihood depended solely on patronage. Everyone admired his literary brilliance, but his poetry boldly celebrated ideas that bordered on heresy, and he had enemies among the rigorously orthodox who "blacklisted" him whenever they came to power. Periodically, he would fall out of favor and lose his position, both at court and in the college. He would sometimes use his skills as a copyist to support his family until his fortunes improved. At least once, however, he was forced to leave Shiraz. For several years he lived as an exile, often in dire poverty. Finally a new, more tolerant regime allowed him to return home and resume his career. During the long, unsettled middle period of his life, first his son and later his wife passed away. Some scholars associate many of his deeply felt verses of grief, separation, and loss with these events.

By the time he was sixty, Hafiz had become famous as a master poet. A circle of students and companions gathered around him, and he served them as a teacher and counselor until his quiet death at about the age of seventy. He was buried in one of his favorite spots, at the foot of a cypress tree he himself had planted in a rose garden near Shiraz. For five hundred years his tomb, surrounded by the rose garden, was a center of pilgrimage and refreshment for thousands. By the early twentieth century, however, the tomb had fallen into disrepair. Then, in 1925, arrangements were made with the Persian government to have a new structure built over the grave and to have the gardens gradually restored. These arrangements were initiated and partially funded by a contemporary spiritual figure from India who loved Hafiz, Avatar Meher Baba. This modern world teacher frequently quoted couplets of Hafiz to illustrate his own discussions of spiritual principles. Meher Baba explained that the love poetry of Hafiz contained all the secrets of the spiritual path—for the true subject matter of spirituality is Love.

SPIRITUAL STUDENT

We have been in love with God
For so very, very long.

Hafiz was, in fact, a spiritual student. As a young man, he became a disciple of a Sufi teacher who guided him through a difficult spiritual apprenticeship that lasted most of his adult life. Later, Hafiz himself became a Sufi master. His *Divan* (collected poems) is a classic in the literature of Sufism, an ancient spiritual tradition whose special emphasis is intense, often ecstatic, one-pointed devotion to God.

In the West, Sufism is usually regarded as a form of Islamic mysticism. However, the Sufis themselves say their "way" has always existed, under many names, in many lands, associated with the mystical dimension of every spiritual system. In ancient Greece, for example, they were identified with the wisdom *(sophia)* schools of Pythagoras and Plato. At the time of Jesus, they were called Essenes or Gnostics. After Muhammad, they adopted many of the principles and formulations of Islam and became known in the Muslim world as "Sufis," a word given various meanings, including "wisdom," "purity," and "wool" (for the coarse woolen habits of wandering dervishes).

From about 800 to 1400 A.D., Sufi schools flourished under the guidance of master teachers such as Rumi and Ibn Arabi. As individual schools developed, their methods of teaching diversified according to the needs of each group. Some stressed formal meditation, others focused on selfless service to the world, and still others emphasized devotional practices: song, dance, and spiritual poetry celebrating love for God. The Sufis cherish the poetry of Hafiz as a perfect expression of the human experience of divine love.

How Hafiz came to be a Sufi student is a famous and popular story told in many versions throughout the East:

It is said that when he was twenty-one and working as a baker's assistant, Hafiz delivered some bread to a mansion and happened to catch a fleeting glimpse of a beautiful girl on the terrace. That one glimpse captured his heart, and he fell madly in love with her, though she did not even notice him. She was from a wealthy noble family, and he was a poor baker's assistant. She was beautiful, he was short and physically unattractive—the situation was hopeless.

As months went by, Hafiz made up poems and love songs celebrating her beauty and his longing for her. People heard him singing his poems and began to repeat them; the poems were so touching that they became popular all over Shiraz.

Hafiz was oblivious of his new fame as a poet; he thought only of his beloved. Desperate to win her, he undertook an arduous spiritual discipline that required him to keep a vigil at the tomb of a certain saint all night long for forty nights. It was said that anyone who could accomplish this near-impossible austerity would be granted his heart's desire. Every day Hafiz went to work at the bakery. Every night he went to the saint's tomb and willed himself to stay awake for love of this girl. His love was so strong that he succeeded in completing this vigil.

At daybreak on the fortieth day, the archangel Gabriel appeared before Hafiz and told him to ask for whatever he wished. Hafiz had never seen such a glorious, radiant being as Gabriel. He found himself thinking, "If God's messenger is so beautiful, how much more beautiful must God be!" Gazing on the unimaginable splendor of God's angel, Hafiz forgot all about the girl, his wish, everything. He said, "I want God!"

Gabriel then directed Hafiz to a spiritual teacher who lived in Shiraz. The angel told Hafiz to serve this teacher in every way and his wish would be fulfilled. Hafiz hurried to meet his teacher, and they began their work together that very day.

HAFIZ AND HIS TEACHER

Our Partner is notoriously difficult to follow,
And even His best musicians are not always easy
To hear.

The teacher's name was Muhammad Attar. *Attar* signifies a chemist or perfumer, and it is believed that Muhammad Attar owned a shop in Shiraz and lived a very ordinary public life. Only his small circle of students knew him as a spiritual teacher.

Hafiz visited Attar nearly every day for years. They sat together, sometimes dined together, sometimes talked, sometimes sang, sometimes went for quiet walks in the beautiful rose gardens of Shiraz. Attar opened Hafiz's vision to fresh, ever deeper perceptions of the beauty and harmony of life and a much broader understanding of all the processes of love. It was natural for Hafiz to express these insights in the language of poetry. Muhammad Attar was also a poet, and he encouraged Hafiz in this direction. For many years, Hafiz created a poem a day for his teacher. Attar told his students to collect and study these poems, for they illustrated many of the central principles of spiritual unfolding.

However, the relationship between Hafiz and his teacher was not always an easy one. In many accounts, Muhammad Attar is presented as a stern and demanding figure who sometimes appeared to show no compassion at all for Hafiz. Modern spiritual figures, notably Avatar Meher Baba, have used the example of Hafiz and Attar to illustrate how challenging and difficult it can be to serve an authentic spiritual teacher. In his discourses on the role of the master, Meher Baba explains that, regardless of external appearances, a teacher must always aid internal processes of growth that support increasingly broader designs of love. Along the way, the student's limited ego is dissolved—or, as Hafiz says, ground to dust. Meher Baba described this process as "hell on earth" for Hafiz. He said, "Hafiz, so to speak, broke his head at the feet of his master," day after day, year after year, for forty long years.

Some stories about Hafiz and his teacher support this view. Often Hafiz is portrayed as running to Attar in despair, pleading for enlightenment or spiritual liberation after decades of frustration. Each time, Attar would tell Hafiz to be patient and wait, and all would be revealed. According to one account:

One day, when Hafiz was well over sixty, he confronted his aged teacher and said, "Look at me! I'm old, my wife and son are long dead. What have I gained by being your obedient disciple for all these years?" Attar gently replied, "Be patient and one day you will know. " Hafiz shouted, "I knew I would get that answer from you!" In a fever of spiritual desperation, he began another form of forty day vigil. This time he drew a circle on the ground and sat within it for forty days and nights, without leaving it for food, drink, or even to relieve himself. On the fortieth day, the angel again appeared to him and asked what he desired. Hafiz discovered that during the forty days all his desires had disappeared. He replied instantly that his only wish was to serve his teacher.

Just before dawn Hafiz came out of the circle and went to his teacher's house. Attar was waiting at the door. They embraced warmly, and Attar gave Hafiz a special cup of aged wine. As they drank together, the intoxicating joy of the wine opened his heart and dissolved every trace of separateness. With a great laugh of delight, Hafiz was forever drowned in love and united with God, his divine Beloved.

It is said that Hafiz unknowingly began his vigil exactly forty days before the end of his fortieth year of service to his teacher and that the "moment of union" was exactly forty years to the day from the moment they first met.

LEVELS OF LOVE

All I know is Love,
And I find my heart Infinite
And Everywhere!

Many of these vignettes about Hafiz have the charming symmetry and precision of symbolic teaching stories. The recurring number forty, for example, might not be meant literally. In spiritual literature, "forty" is often used to indicate a term of learning or change, such as the "forty days and forty nights" of Noah's Flood. Forty is also called "the number of perseverance," marking a period of growth through testing, trial, and purification. After the exodus from Egypt, the Israelites endured "forty years of wandering" in the wilderness before they were ready to enter the Promised Land. Jesus, following the ancient practice of the prophets, went into the desert for a great seclusion of forty days, which he described as a period of purification and preparation for the next stage of his work. The Buddha attained final enlightenment after forty days of continuous meditation. One can find many examples, East and West.

These tales of Hafiz share other common symbols. There is the "mystic circle," which is an image of completion or perfection. And there is the glass of wine Attar gives Hafiz. A glass or cup is a vessel, which can often represent the human heart, or even the human being as a vessel of love. "Wine" stands for love in many spiritual traditions. Aged wine, such as Attar shares with Hafiz, can represent the purified (distilled) essence of knowing or love.

As teaching stories, these episodes can be seen to illustrate central stages of the Sufi "path of love" or inner unfolding:

Hafiz begins his spiritual journey as nearly everyone does—he is awakened to love. An ideal of human beauty and perfection seizes his heart. Desperate to win his ideal, he fully explores the realm of human love (his poems and songs celebrate her beauty and his longing for her).

Finally, he directs all the energies of his life to the pursuit of love (a forty-day vigil).

When his longing reaches its highest pitch (dawn of the final day), *a new and higher dimension of love reveals itself* (Gabriel). *He is able to respond to the beauty of this higher understanding* ("I want God!"), *and his response ushers him into a new phase of learning and a new relationship of love* (with a spiritual teacher).

This new term of growth (forty years) *is exponentially longer than the first one. Attar leads Hafiz through a review of increasingly broader and more encompassing levels of love* (a poem a day). *Hafiz becomes restless as his love for God grows stronger. Attar constantly counsels "patience" to remind Hafiz that every stage of love must be fully explored, honored, and lived.*

As the term nears its end, Hafiz reaches a new height of desperation and longing for his Beloved. He again seeks to devote all his energies to love (another forty-day vigil). *This time he binds himself within a circle* (of perfection or completion), *literally circumscribing all his thoughts and actions to a single focus—God. He strives to perfect his love for God until nothing else exists for him.*

When he has truly accomplished this (dawn of the final day), *he finds that the force of love has consumed his limited personality and all its desires, even the desire for God. He has realized that one cannot "master" love, one can only serve as a vessel of love* (a glass of wine).

Emerging from the circle, Hafiz is now able to approach and embrace every experience of life with the unlimited wisdom of love (he and his teacher embrace). *He and Attar now share the same perfect knowing* (the aged wine of love's maturity). *The "glass of aged wine" now becomes a symbol for "the embodiment of perfect love"—Hafiz himself.*

PERFECTION

I hear the voice
Of every creature and plant,
Every world and sun and galaxy—
Singing the Beloved's Name!

The idea that a human being can achieve "perfect love" or "perfect knowing" may seem extraordinary, yet it is a belief shared by most spiritual systems. It is called by many names—union with the Father, *nirvikalpa samadhi*, the highest development of consciousness, God-realization, *Qutubiyat*, or simply Perfection. One who attains it can be called a Perfect Master, someone who embodies a perfect understanding of the beauty and harmony of the universe.

A Perfect Master experiences life as an infinite and continuous flow of divine love, swirling in, around and through all forms of life and all realms of creation. It is an experience of total unity with all life and all beings. A Perfect Master personifies perfect joy, perfect knowing, and perfect love and expresses these qualities in every activity of life.

In the Western world, the most familiar example of such perfect love may be Francis of Assisi. In the East, there have been many— Rumi in Persia, Kabir and Ramakrishna in India, Milarepa in Tibet, Lao-tzu in China are all revered as Perfect Masters.[*]

The teacher of Hafiz, Muhammad Attar, was a Perfect Master, and so was Hafiz himself. The poetry of Hafiz can be read as a record of a human being's journey to perfect joy, perfect knowing, and perfect love.

MASTER POET

Write a thousand luminous secrets
Upon the wall of existence
So that even a blind man will know
Where we are,
And join us in this love!

Hafiz developed his poetry under the guidance of his teacher. Muhammad Attar reviewed and discussed the poems in his teaching circle, and many of them were set to music. This was a common practice in Sufi schools of the time, including Rumi's order of "whirling dervishes" in Turkey. Poetry and song, easy to memorize and repeat, were used as teaching materials to encapsulate or summarize spiritual principles. With Attar's encouragement, Hafiz perfected this teaching method using a popular form of love song, the *ghazal*. He wrote hundreds of *ghazals*, finding ways to bring new depth and

---

[*] 'World Teachers such as Jesus, Buddha, Krishna, and Muhammad also exemplify perfection—Personified.

meaning to the lyrics without losing the accustomed association of a love song.

His poems expressed every nuance and stage of his growing understanding of love. He wrote of the game of love, the beauty of the Beloved, the sweet pain of longing, the agony of waiting, the ecstatic joy of union. He explored different forms and levels of love: his delight in nature's beauty, his romantic courtship of that ideal unattainable girl, his sweet affection for his wife, his tender feelings for his child, and his terrible grief and loneliness when, later in his life, both his wife and his son passed away. He wrote of his relationship with his teacher and his adoration of God.

All who heard his poetry could easily associate it with their own most cherished experiences of love. The familiar rhythms of the love-song, the *ghazal*, made the poems easy to learn. Before long, his poems were sung all over Persia by people from every walk of life—farmers, craftsmen, scholars, princes, even children.

Many who knew of Hafiz and enjoyed his poetry had no idea that he was a Sufi. Nor did many people know the spiritual status of his teacher. Like many Sufi masters of his time, Muhammad Attar met with his students in secret, and Hafiz did not reveal his own association with Attar until after his master's death. In the religious climate of medieval Persia, this secrecy was essential. From time to time, waves of what might be called fanatical fundamentalism swept through the country. To these fundamentalists, it was blasphemy to suggest that any human being could attain perfection or approach direct knowledge of divinity. The Sufi schools were frequently outlawed, and many of their adherents were tried and executed. Those who survived were forced to meet in secret and disguise their teachings in a symbolic language that would not offend the orthodox. This became the language of Sufi poetry. Images of wine and the Tavern came to represent love and the Sufi school; the nightingale and the Rose were the lover and the Beloved. Spiritual students were depicted as clowns, beggars, scoundrels, rogues, courtesans, or intoxicated wayfarers.

This symbolic language developed gradually over hundreds of years. Hafiz brought it to perfection in his poetry. Even today, people argue about the "true" meaning of his verses—is he simply describing the joy of walking in the garden or speaking symbolically about God's delight in the material forms of His Creation? Or both? When he praises a wealthy patron or the charms of a young woman, is he really celebrating God, his true Patron and Beloved? Perhaps both. For Hafiz does not see God as separate from the world—wherever there is love, there is the Beloved. The Indian Sufi teacher Inayat Khan explained, "The mission of Hafiz was to express to a fanatical religious world that the presence of God is not to be found only in heaven, but also here on earth."

In Persian, Hafiz is sometimes called the Tongue of the Invisible, for so many of his poems seem to be ecstatic and beautiful love songs from God to His beloved world. Hafiz shares his intoxication with the magic and beauty of divine life that pulsates everywhere around us and within us. He urges us to rise on the wings of love. He challenges us to confront and master the strongest forces of our own nature. He encourages us to celebrate even the most ordinary experiences of life as precious divine gifts. He invites us to "awake awhile" and listen to the delightful music of God's laughter.

> What is this precious love and laughter
> Budding in our hearts?
> It is the glorious sound
> Of a soul waking up!

JANUARY

LISTEN TO THIS MUSIC

I am a hole in a flute that the Christ's breath
moves through—listen to this music.

I am the concert from the movement of every
creature singing in myriad chords.

And every dancer, their foot I know and lift.
And every brush and hand, well, that is me
too, who caresses any canvas or cheek.

How did I become all these things, and beyond
all things?

It was my destiny, as it is yours. My poems are
about our glorious journey.

We are a hole in a flute, a moment in space, that
the Christ's body can move through and sway

all forms—in an exquisite dance—as the wind in
a forest.

SO YOU CAN PLANT MORE WHEAT

I would like to remove some rocks from your
field so that you can plant more wheat.

And those hills I see that are part of you, I
have some trees in mind for them

and flowering grasses, so that you won't erode
when the elements pour.

Are we not lovers? Cannot I speak to you like
this?

Do I need to ask your permission to hitch up
my ox and sing to him as I improve your vast
terrain?

The title to your heart came to my office. In
looking at it a great interest in your soul
developed. The care of your soul became mine.

So I would like to remove some stones from
your meadows; then an orchard you could grow,

and the world, and the world then, will come
to taste your riches.

CAN ANY BEAUTY MATCH THIS?

When the sun within speaks, when love
reaches out its hand and places it upon
another,

any power the stars and planets might
have upon us,

any fears you can muster can become so
rightfully insignificant.

What one heart can do for another heart,
is there any beauty in the world that can
match this?

Brotherhood, sisterhood, humanity becomes
the joy and the emancipation.

BATTING 900

I once walked around with a sign on my back.
The reason for this was

that upon analysis I came to the conclusion
that about 90% of what anyone had to say
was some kind of sales pitch.

So whenever anyone would start to talk to me
I would just turn around and let them read
my written reply, my sign, which said . . .

Nothing Doing.

Nine times out of ten I was right. Who goes
through life as well as that . . . batting 900!

WHAT THE PROM QUEEN GETS

Time an enemy not easy to slay. It can tear
the wing apart, sever it with such an unclean
cut one can bleed for days.

An hour is a clever hallucination, a year more
so, a lifetime . . . the grand hoax.

The way sound and light travel, the way all
come from a source that has never moved,

at the height of the action of longing or in the
perfect resistance to all the forces of morals . . .
everything can stop.

That is where you want to be, where the clock's
tyranny has lost its influence.

One always gets a big prize for that—for any
intelligent, overall functional, useful deductions.

The door prize is, heaven wraps itself in a box
and places itself at your feet.

With such a door prize, try to imagine what the
prom queen gets.

JANUARY 6

LET'S EAT

Why just show you God's menu?
Hell, we are all starving.

L
E
T'
S

E
A
T

COULD BE LIFTED

If you knew the end of your story, nothing on
any page—*not one of your* dramas, could bother
you as much.

If you knew the glorious end of your journey,
at least half of your attention could be lifted
from anything you can now focus on that may
cause you pain.

His hand is like that, when it is realized near,
it will always turn your gaze in the direction
of more light.

WHEN THE VIOLIN

When the violin can forgive the past it
starts singing.

When the violin can stop worrying
about the future

you will become such a drunk laughing
nuisance

the Sun will then lean down and start
combing you into its hair.

When the violin can forgive every wound
caused by others

your soul, your soul will start singing.

KNOW THE TRUE NATURE

Know the true nature of your Beloved.
In His loving eyes your every thought,

word, and movement is always, always,
beautiful.

LESS INCLINED TO DRINK

She kissed the best, a dog I knew, and there
were infinitely fewer complications;

thus, at the end of the day I felt less inclined
to drink.

Knowing it is to our advantage to never belittle
anything

I feel I should say something positive about
human lips:

I had some fine moments with them, we tried,
we tangoed from different angles,

but I like my affections and investments of time
to be appreciated enough on an ongoing basis

to see a pretty tail always wag.

INHERENT IN SUFFERING

Inherent in most suffering, especially that
of the mind or heart,

is feeling, is believing that you can miss
something in life.

But that is not true. For on your wedding
day with the Sun,

one of His presents to you will be—if you
want it—every experience that has ever
been known or can be known.

Yes, a divine treasury awaits each soul. It is
the INFINITE, infinite possibilities, that

you can really borrow from at any moment,
right now.

WHEN HIS FOOT TOUCHES EARTH NEAR ME

Not like a lone beautiful bird, these poems
now rise in great white flocks, startled by
God,

breaking a branch, when His foot touches
earth . . . *near me.*

Not like a lone beautiful bird need be your
heart when I am close, like this.

THE SALMON RUN

I wonder how God ever gets any work done
when He could just be gazing at Himself
in awe all day? What discipline He shows.

I am talking about a real problem that will
challenge you someday, though you may
know nothing about that yet:

splendor taking over the place and rising
from your body like a sunrise—gods sitting
on a hill needing to bask in you. For it is true,
we help sustain existence.

All types of fishermen, merchants and seekers
will gather around you when you reach your
goal.

They will be wanting to cast their nets into
the brilliant salmon run you become,

leaping into the sky, offering to take any near
along.

GOD IS APPLAUDING

God is applauding our every act, but
He hides that reality from most, until
we can understand more about real

love.

A LEGITIMATE QUESTION & FEELING COMPELLED

What do lovers do after their bodies have
performed all the little magic that they can,

after the enchantment of limb-caressing love
created such a force and shelter of protection

the world was held at bay for precious moments,
and the future and the past waited as it always
does outside a seer's house, humbly,

in some shed out back where the garden tools
are kept, and then lifted by the real teacher if
ever she or he desires

to plant something in time's meadow that can
benefit generations?

Hey, that looks like one sentence up *north*. I
rarely write like that knowing most have a short
attention span, and may feel compelled to check
some message.

That long sentence looks too *windy* to proofread
and it might have gotten more cerebral than I
intended and or esoteric. In short, good luck in
contemplating that one . . . if you try.

Nevertheless, I think I pose a legitimate question . . .
about lovers passing time, and magic tools you have
in a shed.

LIKE ON THAT LAST DITTY

In every line I have left a gold coin, an emerald,

a bone still with some meat on it, or a key to
a place you want to enter.

If you ever read something of mine and think,
I just don't get it,

maybe your brain is having an off day. It is
not my fault . . .

I double-checked—many times—everything
I have ever written . . . even if I say otherwise,
like on that last ditty.

Be like the one who digs if need be, trusting
that I am not fooling around.

Something of great worth in my pocket wants
to be in yours.

WATCH OUT FOR SPIRITUAL LA-LA LAND

Watch out for spiritual la-la land, where you might
wind up comatose.

Some early warning signs are:

A. You start wearing all orange or white and count
your beads in public.

B. You chant something mysterious in Sanskrit
or some language from another planet while
burning incense that (unknown to you) is laced
with potent hash, that makes you think you are on
the right track when naked devas start appearing.

C. You start believing some basically regular guy
or gal with dreamy eyes—who parrots wisdom—
is *a saint.*

D. Even with those imaginary devas running
around (who you would have thought might have
stimulated your lower chakras), your wife or
husband or lovers start to think: Gosh, what
happened to my sweetheart? We used to do it in the
car, in traffic jams, behind our tinted windows to
pass the time constructively, and now look, yes,
now just look . . . my sweetheart hasn't gone down
on me in three months, and may never again.

E. Your high school graduating class pitches
in for the best *cult deprogrammer* in the world for
you, as a birthday present. Especially if you were
a runner-up, or ever even remotely considered
most likely to succeed.

THE SKINNED KNEE IS BETTER OFF

Since the Beloved is involved in everything, it has
to be this way:

The skinned knee is better off for having ached.

And a face that has known a tear's movement,
it may not show right away any signs of change,

but a magnificent inner canyon is being formed
from the currents of sacred elements touching—
shaping us.

When will tenderness reign? When will love govern?
There is a court you rule that affects any you near,
so you tell me.

Something became apparent a while back: Listening
to others deeply is vital to human development.

The heart cannot deny the law of action and reaction.
It will give in proportion to what it has cherished.

Some great thermal force is within us that can warm
and comfort many. Clever bargaining is legal on the
path, it can help light come into your possession.
All is a means to God.

The skinned knee is better off for having yelped,
but I consider where I step so I do not trip upon
or harm another.

The hand will give in proportion to what the eye has
seen. So study my face, share the bounty of other
worlds in a look my countenance holds.

WHEN MY REAR END BECOMES
AS CUTE AS MARS

Sometimes I am like a big firefly, suspended in
midair because of ecstasy.

When my rear end becomes as cute as Mars—
uncontrollably blinking, winking, wishing
goodwill to the earth from the sky—

it is hard to stay incognito (as is my preference)
and not have someone point toward me and say,

"Hey, look at Hafiz."

What to do? I guess illumination is hard to hide!

WHY YOU STARE AT THE MOUNTAIN

What does real love do? It stills the longing, for real
love is crowned, and then all become its willing slave.

Love creates a home wherever it is. Love is really
never in want. True love is always in a state of *found*.

Homeless one is, whenever the heart is not alive.
Realizing that, I sing the way I do. A bird's melody
can grant a pardon to vision that is obstructed.

I know why you stare at the mountain's beauty,
for she reminds you of something vital in your self.
And natural desires to explore her heights are just
there to help your reach your own summit.

Once, while I was looking at the sky, it spoke, saying,
"Hafiz, I am surprised at your admiration for me,
for dear you are my root. With a ruby in your purse
why wish to hold a clay coin?"

I like this poem, its weave. It is a basket where
something has been placed for you. Read this again,
slowly, it may become more revealed.

A problem has arisen. I can't leave right now, you
feel too close. Do you mind if we kiss for an hour?

THEY ARE HOLDING A BALL

When there is a lot of confusion, the result is
usually sadness. Clarity and order, what is their
worth, what follows them?

Any congested lanes of traffic inside come to
a halt, carriages are abandoned and moved off
the road, horses get turned out to graze in the
firmament.

Freed from maintenance of small spaces and
petty things, something might raise your chin—
an invisible arm, your dimension can shift.

And the wonders you forgot are still there waiting
to play.

There is an expanded field where all things are ever
new. All objects there are holding a ball they wish
to toss,

just wanting you to have some lighthearted fun,
catching light.

I BET WE CAN FIGURE SOMETHING OUT

How many times do you need to hear *who you are*
before you begin to cash *some* of that in and stop
acting like a beggar . . . for any kind of attention
from people who do not really love you?

Sweeping the streets the way that some do, with
eyes that might covet, is no longer fitting to us.
For we are everything's lord.

There is no pride on my face, just the opposite.
For I got to this great position in making myself
ready every moment to serve another.

All the alertness any creature might know, all
primal strength and agility, I would use if we
were near . . . to care for you in a way a divine
lion would its cub.

I don't want you to leave me and go back into any
world that can frighten. What can I do? I bet we
can figure something out.

WORD SPREADS ABOUT GOOD COOKING

The movements of our hands help build the
Unseen.

We add to the universe by our efforts.
Whatever we do, we should never think it is
irrelevant;

whatever we do, we should not conclude it
is so important either. Between those two

poles find your balance; between those two
regions your talents will bloom.

Word spreads about good cooking. Become
that, an exquisite meal for us.

The alchemy stone is waiting to retire and
confess . . . *something in us is its power.*

JUST IN CASE YOU SLIP

Few can escape self-made traps.

And when a person falls into one, it is
natural to call out for help.

If you attend such a plea, take someone
like me along as a safety rope or ladder . . .

just in case you slip.

CERTAINTY

From man's perspective in this extraordinary
game of life

it is so easy to become confused and think
you are the *doer*,

but from God's infinite certainty He always
knows

He is the only One who should ever be put
on trial.

INTO YOUR UNDIES

How long will you remain content just
to hear and tell stories of what happens
beyond your horizons,

where the courageous had no choice but
to live their ideals and imbibe effulgence's
shape?

Restlessness and a lack of peace can play
a vital part in your inner unfoldment.

If you ever become too complacent, too
accepting of your sorrow or shadow self,

the moon might fling a beehive into your
undies and that should wake you up.

DISSOLVING IN THE INFINITE

I have opened all the windows in my house.
Eagles fly in and out, as do any words that
are spoken about me.

Anything my ears might detect, firsthand or
second . . . I might give that news a moment's
attention

and then just let it be the tiny evaporating
whiff of smoke it is, dissolving in the Infinite.

EVERY HOLY BOOK

A candle giving advice to the sun can
make the sun smile because of the flame's
remarkable innocence.

Maybe I should be careful about saying
something like this, but every holy book . . .

lifts the corners of my mouth, and even
makes me giggle a bit.

ALL IN ALL

"Could you help me with this?" an ant said
to an elephant when a large seed the ant was
dragging back to its nest got stuck between
some grass.

The elephant, looking down and feeling
kindhearted that day, began to contemplate
all that might be needed to render some
service,

but the task just seemed too delicate and
in need of more precision than the elephant's
trunk or one of his feet or even his tail or one
of his grand ears could handle effectively.

So the elephant began to pray for divine
intervention, and sure enough it worked, or
it seemed to—

a berry on a nearby bush happened to fall in
such a way as to free the seed for its onward
destination.

The elephant's faith in God was increased,
and the ant, having heard the prayer, was
now less of an agnostic, which he had been
for the last year or so because of personal
reasons . . . he would rather keep private.

All in all, seems things are moving ahead,
working out for the best. Yep.

DON'T LOOK SHORTCHANGED

You can return to Springtime whenever you want.

And your greatest pleasures, don't let their
memory ever fade; let them be as they should, a
genuine guide and friend,

ever there to take you back again to what made
you happy once—or brought you deeper into the
Heart.

Wanting to be other than where you are—who
cursed you like that? Break that spell.

Wherever you might wind up after your body is
buried, cremated, left at the Tower of Silence,
or set floating down the Ganges,

anywhere your soul might someday call home,
come to your senses—you carry that inside now,
so don't look shortchanged.

Things can only appear dismal until that one eye
opens and the sacred flame makes you squint.

You can return to the Divine Season at a flex
of your will's might, and be the luminous sphere
in the sky, raining on us, as it does.

ONCE A YOUNG WOMAN SAID TO ME

Once a young woman said to me, "Hafiz, what
is the sign of someone who knows God?"

I became very quiet, and looked deep into her
eyes, then replied,

"My dear, they have dropped the knife. Someone
who knows God has dropped the cruel knife

that most so often use upon their tender self
and others."

FEBRUARY

ONE REGRET

One regret, dear world, that I am determined
not to have when I am lying on my deathbed
is that I did not kiss you enough.

WHAT MADNESS IS AUSTERITY

What madness is austerity in the rose season! When the sky
meadow blooms so should we. And in winter, why can't the warmth
of any summer day still be on our faces, that another can feel.

You have tied heaven's hands behind her back and veiled her
face, otherwise her lips you would know any hour you desired.

Write a little note to yourself about when your heart was most
alive. Carry that with you for a fortnight;

some tiny transference of love could happen to all you near,
when your memory touches what was once sacred to you.

Anything good in your past is a harbinger of what is to come
in greater quantities.

Some words of Saadi* come to mind about this—why should
they not when he was such an influence upon me.

He helped me grow from child to man; he helped my arms
embrace others more deeply. He increased my pen's abilities
every time I bowed and sang at his tomb.

"Whatever beauty you have known, darling, you will know a
thousand times more."

Whatever beauty you have known, you will know a thousand times
more.

---

* Saadi Shirazi, Sheikh Mosleh al-Din (c. 1184–1283), better known as Saadi, was
one of the major Persian poets of the medieval period. He is recognized not only for
the quality of his writing but also for the depth of his social thought. A famous poem
of his is displayed in the United Nations building in New York. President Obama, in
2009, recited this poem for the commemoration of Nowruz, the Persian New Year.

I LEFT FIREWOOD *&* SMOOCHING

There is a disease I know, it is called: being too serious.

Don't worry, you won't catch it from my poems.

I let eloquence have its say, and wisdom too and mirth, for they can be needed companions as you navigate this dimension and others.

Wherever you have dreamed of going, I have camped there, and left firewood for when you arrive.

Try this someday: When you are packing or moving any simple object around—imagine your Beloved's

hand—as yours. And it then might *become thus*, if just for a second.

But a wondrous, true moment like that would be enough for the integration to begin,

the meld of you and light . . . and then the smooching, the wild smooching all the time. Why not?

WANTING OUR LIFE TO MAKE SENSE

All day long you do this, and then even in your
sleep . . . *pan for gold.*

We are looking to find something to celebrate
with great enthusiasm,

wanting all our battles and toil and our life to
make sense.

"I found it, I found it, I found it!" a hermit once
began to shout, after having spent years in
solitude, meditating.

"Where?" a young shepherd boy nearby asked.
"Where?"

And the hermit replied, "It may take a while,
but I will show you. For now, just sit near to me."

All day long we do this with our movements
and our thoughts . . . pan for gold.

TOSS A PALACE YOUR WAY

Looks like you are doing not so bad for being
under the gun as you are.

I mean, you have not spent too much time
locked up—in any kind of jail have you?

Aren't you able to walk about like a basically,
free-range chicken?

They haven't attached any radar sensors
to you yet, have they? That is a good sign,

that seems a clear vote of confidence from
society.

Hold out a little longer. Luck may shift
your way even more. Someone like Hafiz may

ask you to do a small favor. If so, carry that
out as if some great king had assigned you a
royal errand,

and might then toss a palace your way for a job
well done.

IT WAS BEAUTIFUL ONE NIGHT

It was beautiful, it was so beautiful one night
we all began to expect God would speak

from the waves reaching toward the millet
fields,

from the mouths of the hanging sky
ornaments crooning in light's infinite codes,

from the glances of children and plants
and hills playing with effulgent life.

It was beautiful, it was so beautiful one night
we all began to expect God would speak.

AN INFANT IN YOUR ARMS

The tide of my love has risen so high,
let me flood over you.

Close your eyes for a moment and
maybe all your fears and fantasies
will end.

If that happened God would become
an infant in your arms

and then you would have to nurse
all creation.

HOW DO I LISTEN?

How do I listen to others? As if everyone were my Master speaking to me his cherished last words.

How do I listen to you? As if you were the Alpha and Omega of all sound.

WHEN THE STOCK MARKET TAKES A HIT

Contemplate this over some morning coffee
or tea, or when the stock market takes a big hit:

*Zero is where the real fun starts; there is too much
counting everywhere else!*

IMAGINATION DOES NOT EXIST

For me, and for the one who is One with God,
imagination does not exist.

Whatever you might be able to do in a dream,
or in thought or fantasy,

I could literally pull from my pocket, or just
make appear in my hand.

What kind of world is this then that we live
in?

It has been *make-believe* since the beginning
and does not know any other way to act.

WHERE IS THE DOOR TO THE TAVERN?

Where is the door to God?
In the sound of a barking dog,

in the ring of a hammer, in a drop
of rain, in the face of everyone,
everyone I see.

Where is the door to the divine
tavern? Yes, in all we can behold.

THE BODY A TREE

The body a tree, God a wind.
When He moves me like this, like this,

angels bump heads with each other
gathering beneath my cheeks,

holding their wine barrels, catching
the brilliant tear, pearl rain.

Love, a tree. When it moves us like this.
How can our soul's limbs not touch?

RETIRE IN THE ALPS

The great religions are the ships,
poets the lifeboats.

Every sane person I know has
jumped overboard!

Hafiz, that is good for business,
isn't it? Indeed,

but I would rather retire in the Alps!

ONE OUTGROWS CHOICE

No one but a rebel can get their mitts on God.
And at some point you will have to wean yourself
from the pack. Wish the cares of others well.

If you really want to do something for those you
love, want to leave a lasting legacy for this world,

you need to climb higher, or reach deeper within
and what you then find, well . . .

well, you won't need to think about what to do
with it; free will is an illusion.

God spoke your every word in His mind before
your birth. And one movement of His hand
contained your every act.

There is an Infinite Knowledge that has always
existed, and in it resides everything. And *that* will
someday dawn on you, for you are the Infinite's
heir.

Real Knowing never makes love to choice, or even
considers the un-predestined an option.

For *maybe* and *choice . . . are worlds one outgrows.*
Still, fire burns; and who is not careful around it?

AN APPLE TREE WAS CONCERNED

An apple tree told me it was concerned about
a late frost and losing its gift that would help
feed a poor family close by.

And then there were the jams and lots of
apple butter that could be made in a banner
crop year

when the clouds were generous with what
fell from them and the sun rationed itself
with precision.

They can speak, trees, they can say the sweetest
things, and can even tell a joke,

but it takes special ears to hear them, ears
that have listened to people . . . with great
care.

THE STAIRWAY OF EXISTENCE

We are not in pursuit of formalities or fake
religious laws,

for through the stairway of existence we have
come to God's door.

We are people who need love, because love
is the soul's life, love is simply creation's
greatest joy.

Through the stairway of existence, O through
the stairway of existence, Hafiz,

have you now come, have we now all come,
to the Beloved's door.

THESE CANDLES, OUR BODIES

These candles, our bodies, see how they burn.

How many hours will they last—days, months, years?

Look at the warmth and comfort we can give to each other or to anything that comes close.

One of the components of lasting art is a spirit flame within the created

that can ignite inspiration and hope, and survive time's ways.

STILL THOUGH, WE SHOULD DANCE

A thousand times I have ascertained and
found it to be true:

The affairs of this world are really nothing
into nothing.

Still though, we should dance.

WHO IS LIVING NEXT DOOR?

Who is really living next door to you? To what
extent do you know the answer,

and therefore for a minute now and then . . .
are grateful for their presence?

You have heard about God being indivisible;
is that just a rumor?

Is there a difference between God and existence?

Still, most live as if there are . . . *many in town*,
because slowly we learn.

Some ingredient to solving this vital equation
may be missing.

It could be the physical touch of someone who
knows the Truth.

Someone who knows the Truth and lives it,
the way my Master did,

his touch could bring the fulfillment of prayers.

THE COLOR OF YOUR OCEAN WILL CHANGE

It is possible that just a drop of dye from
a vial the Friend holds could change the color
of an ocean.

I know I have talked about this in different
poems, this basic concept,

but will now say it from a slightly different
angle in case that first arrow I shot completely
missed.

The *presence* of a Perfect One reaches a seed that
is planted in you,

and from that divine warmth, God will lose His
shyness, thaw as it were, and no matter what now,

no matter what you do, the sacred will begin to
grow inside. The color of your ocean will change.

The drop of holy water, the needed dye, has
touched your forehead,

the air did that to you at birth, as did the first
hands that touched you,

and the soft walls—so many times—of your
Mother's womb you lay against.

A SADDLE ON EVERY PARTICLE OF SPACE

Most are still a leaf spinning between heaven and
earth.

What can one see of their surroundings in a state
of fragile or chaotic motion?

Either settle on the ground and come to know
its astounding wonder and sing to us from there,

or maybe sharpen up your meditations and get lifted
higher and reside in the radiant stratosphere

until you turn into such a fine holy ash you integrate
with all.

Put a saddle on every particle of space and ride
like a wild cowboy, and just keep going. Having
fun everywhere,

while you sink your spurs deeper into all Being—
and into what can be called God . . . Who then just
laughs.

DODGING CREDITORS & FEELING HOG-TIED

You might think twice about leaving the sidelines
of love where you are allowed to dawdle.

I wouldn't enter the real playing field unless you
had no other choice. Surely you can come up with
another good excuse.

You could run up some more debt. That could keep
you busy dodging creditors, like a rabbit might the
fox's hunger.

Maybe get a lover on the side, maybe two, maybe
three, that would probably assure a delay in having
to get serious about any inner life for quite a spell,

before you finally decide you do in fact have
to *cough up* some intelligent effort at some point.

What is the value of putting your faith into
practice and concluding there really is something
to all this . . . God stuff?

Well, for openers: It can become a solid wooden
bench you can stand on to see over a hedge that

now keeps your awareness so limited you sometimes
feel hog-tied and wish you were dead.

YOU WILL HAVE TO FACTOR ME IN

Another's sounds should be careful in soliciting
my attention and then my response, unless the

crystal, the Looking Glass, they too wish to enter.

The way a river's strength may move one in its
current, so does my gaze or wish.

What the rain can do for a well, so can the
language from an illumined heart.

When I woke up I found existence rented its
space from me.

I am the wedding partner, every ring, and the
priest who blesses the union.

I am the tenderness that becomes a sacred oath,

thus even when you close the door and might
want privacy,

what can I say? You will still have to factor me
in.

SELLING YOUR ART

At the very least you are a vital cell in a
cosmic holy body.

And everyone works so hard, no matter
what they do.

There is no place for you to go but onward
into a greater freedom.

The poor man rarely parties because of so
many cares. We should put an end to that.

Knowledge can be pawned for a good sum.
Find some truth and mix it with your talents.

If you can get the balance right between you
and others, and you and death, shops will
start selling your art.

And maybe even a masterpiece you will
become, your every gesture.

WHEN THE SUN CONCEIVED A MAN

What could Hafiz utter about that day when
the Sun conceived a man, gave birth to itself
as reality and truth?

What could all the speech in creation ever
say about that resplendent morning when
the eternal Handsome One let his face and
body reappear by grace in form?

There is something I have seen in the interior
of Muhammad that is the luminous root of
all in existence, independent of space and
time's novice dance across a single lute string
of the infinite.

I carry gifts today from the kings of fish, beasts,
birds, and angels. I carry gifts today from rivers,
seas, fields, stars, and from every soul, from
every soul that will ever be.

God, let us know what you first saw that made
you want to do this, create a human heart so in
need.

Let us know, Beloved, that there is only Light.

WHEN ALL THE HAGGLING IS COMPLETE

Don't let that tame-looking lion fool you, that
sweet old man over there.

You think this is an arm and leg you see on me?

He ate those years ago, and crafted these
illusions in their place.

I am talking about that guy, Attar, my master;
I lived close to him for forty years.

"Die before you die," said the Prophet
Muhammad. What do you think that feels like?

It is no game for the fainthearted. It is living
hell,

for there will be nothing left of you but a
molten, bright sphere.

Seems a good trade though, a fantastic deal,
when all the tough haggling is complete.

A GREAT INJUSTICE

It is a great injustice and a monumental act
of cruelty for any religion to make someone
fear God.

THE HAPPY VIRUS

I caught the happy virus again last night
when I was out singing beneath the stars.
It is remarkably contagious, *so kiss me!*

FEBRUARY 29

THE ANOINTMENT

Dear ones, let's anoint this earth with dance!

MARCH

NOTHING LIKE A YESTERDAY

When was the last time you felt complete,
so complete, nothing dared approach you?

Nothing like a yesterday, or a tomorrow.
Nothing that could speak.

Nothing that could ever point to something
that would ever need to be done.

Nothing that could not do anything,
anything but adore you. Adore you. Adore.

LIKE A WINTER COAT

Names have started to admit their inabilities.
I am glad they are being honest.

Honesty always helps; there are fewer chores
then to attend.

Labels shield one from the truth; they are
like a winter coat in a way—

who wants to wear one in this summer we
can spend with you, playing?

IT TRIED TO PREPARE ME

The clear night sky tried to prepare me for
what it knew would someday happen;

it began to show me ever deeper aspects of
its splendor, and then one evening just directly
asked, *Will you be able to withstand your own
magnificence?*

I thought I was just hearing things, until
a spring orchard I was passing my days with

at the height of its glory burst into song,
about our—every human's—destiny to burn
with radiance.

Still I felt my ears were playing tricks on me
until the morning came when God tore apart
my chest . . . needing more room to bloom
inside.

I began to roll through the streets in ecstasy.
Everyone thought I was crazy.

I hope everyone someday knows how blessed
I was. You will.

A GARDEN COULD RISE IN BARREN PLACES

If you don't watch out I just might say something
you will never forget. Then what will you do?

Those words might organize a gang inside your
mind who undertake a strategic plot, or just bully
you to make some changes in your life you have
wanted to make but could not, on your own.

A time-release capsule, my touch and sounds,
with secret instructions hidden within that can
slowly seep into the cracks your heartaches cause.

All of a sudden you might find yourself cleaning
your room more, helping old people across the
street, or giving your money away. Yes, I am
dangerous.

A garden could rise in barren places in you if our
eyes met.

I could turn you into a store that sells shuttle
tickets to other planets; but what use would that
be?

The thing is: I think someone should get more use
out of you for something that will bring pleasure
to others.

It might as well be me who practices some tough
love now and then.

NEVER BE LESS FURRY

I thought God might be willing to listen
to reason, so I worked up a proposal that
outlined some of my many concerns.

My primary objective in that twenty page
thesis of sheer elegance, that I was hoping
might impress Him, could be distilled into
this one, a bit long-winded hoot:

*That you—God—would never be any less
furry, and always as accessible and loving
as my cat; and like her, sleep with your
head on my*

*shoulder. And, of course, don't forget the
purrrrrrrrr!*

A MAN MARRIED TO A BLIND WOMAN

A man married to a blind woman told her how
beautiful she was every day. And whenever he said
that, she smiled, and her whole body relaxed.

They lived alone at a small remote oasis where
few ever stopped. And whenever someone did he
made sure that no one ever saw his wife,

for a person could openly gasp at her appearance
because she was deformed.

Her husband's voice and that of her sister, who
would a few times a year visit, were the only
ones she really knew. And she loved her simple
life on the little farm they had.

Appearances, and our relationship, you should
know the truth of those by now:

If you woke next to me on any day, I would say
to you what he so often did. My dear, you are so
beautiful.

PARALLEL THE CARE THE DANCER TAKES

Parallel the care the dancer takes on her
finest step.

You need to feel the craving for that
unison, you need to know all the
longing the great ones had to suffer

before God said to them, "*Here I am,
yours to do with whatever you like.*"

And when will the Beloved say such
a sublime thing to you, give you all that
power?

A prerequisite is: when all you touch,
you touch as if it were sacred.

That will bring your mind to a standstill.
The space between you and any object

will then open up into a sea of radiance,
where you can drown for a second, drown,
and taste me.

AT THE NILE'S END

We are at the Nile's end, we are carrying
particles from every continent, creature,
and age.

It has been raining on the plains of our
vision for millions of years,

so our senses are a bit muddy compared
to yours, dear God.

But I only hear these words from You
where we are all now trying to embrace
the clear sky ocean,

Dear ones, come. Please, my dear ones come.

GOD COURTS US

God courts us with the beauty of this world.

The Beloved courts us with music, and any touch that quiets,

or can excite to such an extent, one's face will look like a radiant applause.

BASICALLY USELESS

They were happier, all the mouths I saw in a certain city.

For they all woke up one day and mostly forgot what they were for besides . . . just kissing.

And in between their rounds of sweet romantic play, they—all those mouths,

appeared to have few lingering impulses, except for a little food.

That is—talking, everyone came to realize, was basically useless.

MAYBE EVEN ILLEGAL?

Whenever you, God, want to be near me, you are.
Moreover, you can even be more me than I am,
and this, this you always choose.

Something does not seem right here, something
seems unjust and maybe even illegal?

I don't want to have to sic a good lawyer on you,
but I think I have a valid case: I mean, why can't
I be with you the way you are with me?

It is not that I want any kind of power or control
over your domain that a union with you would
bring.

It is just your beauty I so miss, and the way it
makes me alive, feel so alive and at home. Home.

A DAY TOO GREAT A FORCE

Look how the Creator in the form of a mother
or father can then love the created, a child,
even more than themselves.

Look at the salvation and purpose a person
can find in that devotion of caring.

A day is too great a force to bear without the
heart open.

Time will slay your body no matter what, but
with love the impetus of your final movements
will make eloquent your demise.

Could God care for the created more than He
cares for Himself?

The soul, and I think any being, really wants
to love, more than be loved.

IN A HOLY BOOK I HAVE

In a holy book I have there are pages from
the Bible and the Koran.

And pages from the sutras and from the
Upanishads, the Torah, and the Gita.

And pages of things that unknown saints
wrote in collaboration with the heavens
that people have never seen.

And pages of the wisdom of animals and
their young singing while they played, the
way we once did with the stars.

And pages of plants and pages of sounds.
And pages of earths.

Yes, it is all there in my soul, anything ink
has ever preserved, anything that stone ever

begged to have carved on it, anything any
instrument gifted from its mind, or a brush
left for us to see. Any space sanctified by
dance, I know.

And anything that will ever be, written in
your heart. *You*, the eyes or ears and cells
that now hear this.

In a holy book I have, in a sacred text I carry,
is the face of everyone who will ever be.

A TREE YOU CAN WIND AROUND

You are like a wisteria vine in a meadow.
You will naturally climb to the highest point
around as soon as you are able, and then offer
your brilliant color and scents to the world the
best you can when your tendencies ripen enough,
and the temporal and eternal spring dawns.

If a tree were near your arms you would move
toward it as if you were in love, sensing some
potential of giving and receiving more, achieving
your destiny, hanging from the sky, swaying with
the bee-moons happy (us) when your breasts of
light are full of milk . . . when you bloom I mean,
is that not clear? There is so much divinity to
harvest from your glands and your ways of being
when you are kind.

All your limbs, dear, can entwine with a pillar
like me and rise and rise and rise until no one
on earth can see you anymore, for there is no
limit to our height. And any nutrients you
needed I could let flow into your roots and stems,
giving like some umbilical cord that is attached
to my heart.

Continued on March 15th

A TREE YOU CAN WIND AROUND (2)

I am the one always near. There are so many ways to touch me now. If you sing, your sounds will press against my cheek in a way I desire. If you dance I will become the ground you bless, as happiness does this world. And if you make love with another form and can satisfy it, any sighs of respite—*any congratulating noises*—are also mine.

This is just the way things have now become, in short: more delicious our lives. One day, my angel, you will realize you accomplish *everything just by appearing amongst us.*

If I thought you heard what I just said and could cash that in—walk off a wealthy person, I could spare myself repeating it, but I don't mind.

There is really nothing more you can do for us than you having . . . ever been. From a realization came dawn and every benevolent wave that still spreads out exploring the endlessness of time.

THAT SHIELD YOU HOLD

There is a shield you may still hold because of
so many battles.

I guess another conflict could begin any moment,
so maybe lugging it about could be of some use;
or is it just an undermining habit?

Does not it get heavy, so much so that you
sometimes carry it on your head at noon?

And then do wonder, with your insecurities so
intact . . . about casting darkness as fears can
shadows

even if the sun is out, if the *Sun* is out—if God
is really all around in the middle of a beautiful
day or night.

Yes, how amazing that a small umbrella or an
illusion, held over your head . . . or clung to, can
hide the stupendous fact of omniscient Light.

I THINK WE NEED A PASSWORD

I think we need a password, or let's make that a *pass-sentence.*

That way, in case you ever come to my door in an emergency and God and I are busy inside,

we could then just shout, *Tell us the password!* if you really want to snuggle.

And part of the password will be you knowing it is really . . . a pass-sentence. And here it is in all its glory and truth:

Love kicks the ass of time and space.

Upon hearing that God and I would look at each other bewildered, but with delight. We would be glad someone had reached us . . . with the golden key on their tongue.

Though just to make sure we heard you right we might say in unison, *Sing it loudly, baby! Cut loose! We need to double check!*

And then if you did, a strength and smile might rise inside of you, and right next to my heart you might be for a moment . . . beaming like an eye that knows.

Don't forget now: LKTAOTAS.

Maybe even tattoo that somewhere so you will remember.

BECOMING YOUR FACE

Picture the face of your Beloved becoming your
face. And His body fitting on you like a coat
you won't take off again.

Don't move so fast now, when such a rare kiss
is being offered. For what lips can really connect
with a body wired to a mind that is darting about
in a manic hurry?

From this new perspective, look inside the Heart
you have sought so long to be near. Try and go
deep into it. Is it not your own, and mine too?

If for a second all that you want was not just
radiating from your softened eye . . . you best
fire me, or maybe try Rumi, or read this again.

AT BIRTH THE THRONE WAS PROMISED

At birth the throne was promised to the first
son of a king.

A promise that did not even have to be given.
It was simply understood by all in the world
who were aware. It would never be questioned.

And the idea of worth or un-worth never
entered the mind of the prince as he grew,

and it should not enter yours any longer, as
you now take your place, your seat upon the
holy realm again for us.

LEAVE SOMETHING IN THE MARKETPLACE

Sometimes it can happen to these cheeks
when a poem visits my mind for the first time
and begins to look around.

They can wonder why *rain* is falling on them,
and causing my nose to run too.

O boy, what a mess love makes of me. But
there is nothing else right now I would rather

be doing . . . than reaping something from a
field in another dimension

and leaving it in the marketplace for any who
might happen by.

Leave something in the marketplace for us
before you leave this world.

THAT KNOWLEDGE YOU WILL NOT
BE ABLE TO ACCEPT

The parents of three young birds got shot
by a hunter.

After a few days of no food the two largest
birds killed their brother; they ate him and
picked at his bones for a week.

Then that hunger we have all known set in
again, which would cause many to do most
anything, if that ache did last; and it did
and thus other wings never climbed into
the air.

A few more nights passed, and then it was at
sunrise the lone bird fell from its nest, though
it survived on the ground eating some ants,
and then one day it did fly.

Its song came to please many ears, its beauty
enhanced the eye of those who saw it. Even a
loving parent it became.

The guards at the gate of heaven are such
good friends of mine, you should know

there is nothing you have ever done that is
not innocent and will in any way be judged as
wrong by anyone of true wisdom,

but such knowledge you will not be able to
accept until your and an angel's ways are
more similar. It just works like that.

FIRST, THE FISH NEEDS TO SAY

First, the fish needs to say, "Something
ain't right about *this camel ride,*

and

I'm feeling

so

damn

t
h
i
r
s
t
y
!"

SHELTERED BY THE SUN

Look what can grow from one shaft in
a field, or from one shaft like a human
being.

Beautiful cities can rise in our minds
or be burned there to the ground.

We can become so ripe . . . schools and
buildings can be named after us, and
things we have written may come to be
spoken in several tongues.

What does love care about any fame?
Not a thing!

But love does not mind any attention
it gets either, if that attention increases
the capacity to give.

Love does not mind that place where
it camped for a while in a physical form
or where that body may come to rest,

and may even then be revered if that body
became a unique shelter/nourishment for
others.

That is what greatness does: kindly leaves
a shelter for us to gather under, where more
nourishment can be offered to all things.

AS FERTILE AS I AM

Just the deep quiet, just wanting that now, the
unmoving breeze (God) to penetrate me

as if I were a woman needing, wanting, destined
to conceive,

and now was my only moment ever available
to this life when I would be as fertile as I am.

If the Beloved does not lie beside me in the next
hour, if Light does not leave its seed

all over my frame and inside, so full inside that
I drip upon the street

as I then bless the earth with my steps. Another
eon may pass for a conjuncture of the elements in
existence

to be as opportune, as perfect, as all seems now.
But I can't wait, not any longer, knowing how
immaculate . . . the moment.

So I am begging with all my strength, every cell
has joined in and is calling . . . *now, now, now,
now; don't resist us God.*

Continued on March 25th

AS FERTILE AS I AM (2)

And then You are here, the one who sired every
world,

flooding my every crevice, every pore, dissolving
any wound of loneliness, satisfying

every desire . . . eternal and ephemeral, eternal and
ephemeral.

The divine both soothing, making me present, and
tearing me apart, the way true rapture does. This is
what I was really made for.

I will give birth to You now. What else could I
possibly care about?

The world will become my attendant if I ever
asked for anything.

And now look at all the good I could do if I ever
wished.

Yes, we will give birth to You. Listen, Hafiz, to
what you just said. What more could you ever
want?

SACRIFICIAL LAMBS

We are sacrificial lambs offering ourselves to a
false god

if that God does not make it very clear
it wants nothing from us but to share its glory.

And at times, when we really need to know
something about perfection . . .

the movement of your breath might do, or the
beating of our hearts.

MY TEACHER ONCE TOLD ME A STORY

My teacher once told me a story of a great saint,
of a Perfect One, who wanted to travel around
his part of the world before he died and talk about
some spiritual matters to those who would come
to listen.

And when his men and he reached a certain
country he said to some of his companions,

"Sensuality is in fine shape here, maybe even
too fine shape, but my basic concern is that we
fit in well and that we get a few to listen to my
words which will plant seeds here for generations.
So I want you to employ twelve of the most beautiful
erotic dancers who can travel with us for the next
month as we tour this land."

So the dancers were employed, and from town to
town and city to city the great Master traveled.
The dancers would begin the show as it were, and
once a nice crowd had gathered the saint would
speak for just a few minutes, then let the performers
resume their art.

My own Master then stopped the story, looked at
me in a very sweet and somewhat amused way,
then said,

"Hafiz, don't forget the dancers in your poems."

THE ATTRIBUTES OF FINE SPICE

What soup could resist being affected by the
attributes of fine spice,

especially if it were added by the hand of an
excellent cook?

If you memorize some of my words they will
release some of their qualities into your ways.
Friends might say hmmm . . . you taste better,
what happened?

I am not talking about any kind of voodoo.
It is just a fact.

What body would not want to surrender its
tension to a skilled hand, or a pir's words that
can equal any touch?

WE LIVE TO BE NEAR HER

When beauty walks into the room and sits
down close to you and is willing to let you
gaze at her as much as you want,

no one has to tell you all is alright now, no
one has to parrot again . . . someday your pain
won't exist.

For we live to be near her. She oozes grace.
Part of her benediction is that all the hormones
you want to come alive do.

Passion in full throttle says to the past, says to
worries—go fuck yourself, and the past will
crouch down or run . . . like a pup in the
presence of a fierce dog.

When God makes itself more known and all
our attention rivets on some aspect of Splendor,

all our internal dialogue—what can it do, but
cease to deplete one,

then something lifts our heart toward the Sky.

LIE AROUND AND GET ZONKED OUT

If we were smarter, it would have been enough
that just one great Prophet would have to make
a personal appearance on earth.

He or She probably could have easily fixed some
important things forever, written a book that
really gave us the total lowdown . . . and that no
right-wing fanatic dare edit.

God in human form, as some called the Avatar—
or World Teacher—seemingly could have easily
shown us some tasty herb cocktails

that could cure any illness humans would ever
know. But looks like it does not work that way.

And what of us mules who like the harness? What
would the workhorses in this world do without
some imaginary cause—or situation—we felt
needed to be championed, or scotch-taped?

Heaven forbid, everyone might become happy
doing basically nothing

except to lie around and get zonked out on the
wonder of our being.

COMPANION FOR LIFE

Our union is like this: If you feel cold I would
reach for a blanket to cover *our* shivering feet.

If a hunger comes into your body I would run
to my garden and start digging potatoes.

If you asked for a few words of comfort and
guidance I would quickly kneel by your side
and offer you a whole book . . . as a gift.

If you ever ache with loneliness so much you
weep, I would say,

*Here is a rope, tie it around me, Hafiz will be
your companion for life.*

APRIL

WINE IS LIKE THE LORD JESUS

Wine is like the Lord Jesus; it can bring
the dead to life.

IN THE MIDNIGHT OF THY TRESSES

Who can fully renounce a day? Who can conceive
of forgiving a whole life, granting all in it a pardon,

unless at midnight you let us enter your tresses,
know your scent, become as intimate with your
light as anyone ever has.

All images are shadows you did cast. They will
gladly surrender their identity and reveal their

potential the way a piece of paper would if it ever
made love to a great flame.

I HAD A LEGITIMATE EXCUSE

I had a legitimate excuse for not going to the mosque and temple to pray.

It was because love is so wild in me I might break the fragile glass cage that all religions are made of.

MY FAITH INCREASED A BUNCH

When the billboards and neons near God's
inner kingdom started to read with signs
like this—*Piety Not Welcome*—

my faith in God increased a bunch. That is,
I felt a reasonable decoding, a translation of
that message was, *We need to loosen up.*

And those were always my sentiments . . .
exactly.

I NEVER QUITE FEEL RIGHT

I never quite feel right until the effects of
wine reach my head

and kick it back like a mule might
whose hoofs just landed a clean solid blow.

With my vision now corrected and aimed
toward the heavens

and my ticket of intoxication firmly in hand
for at least an hour,

there seem so many interesting possibilities
that I wasn't fully aware of before.

I PROMISE

Has not the Architect, Love, built your heart
in a glorious manner,

with so much care that it is meant to break
if love ever ceases to know all that happens
is perfect?

And where does anything love has ever known
go, when your eye and hand can no longer
be warmed by its body?

So vast a room your soul, every universe can
fit into it.

Anything you once called beautiful, anything
that ever

gave you comfort waits to unite with your
arms again. I promise.

THE COPPER COIN UNDERSTANDS

The copper coin understands its place
amongst the gold.

Any words that can tarnish another know
they are meant to one day be discarded

from your speech, and they will as you
mature, grow ripe and can nourish others
more.

The sounds of pure gold are different than
anything still alloyed; what they say never
in any way harms.

RADIANT IN ITS SHEATH

Outside everyone's house is a great force that
will someday attack.

Many have been carried off, held for some kind
of ransom, mortally wounded, or made
crazed.

Who would raise a child and not prepare him
for such an imminent battle?

Who would ever write a book and not in some
way make you aware of a strong opponent you
will meet?

A sword is most effective if it is never raised,
but can turn radiant in its sheath

and reflect a light onto your face that can still
the anger in others.

ABOUT JUDGMENT DAY

About Judgment Day.

I hope you have come to your senses
and stopped believing everything you
hear.

VISITING A FOREIGN COUNTRY

If you were planning to move to a foreign
country and thought you might never return,

would not it then be prudent to acclimate
yourself to any custom they might have

of say . . . only drinking one certain liquid
and nothing else?

Then, dears, run to the wineshop, run.

For in heaven what can increase your soul's
expanse is all that is ever served.

STAND ALOOF

When a preacher stoops to scare tactics
it is often wise to stand aloof,

for some gods may lose their patience
and start to throw their shoes at him.

CALCULATED MALICE

There is a bird of paradise, Huma, that comes close to earth but never touches the ground.

Sometimes it so nears one has a chance to leap up and touch it.

Those who have received its blessing, from knowing its body firsthand,

all have something in common: Their minds never know any calculated malice, and thus are not weighted down.

JUST AS I SUSPECTED

In a vision I heard this clearly whispered:

Study those who sing the most, but are free of criticism or praise.

Following that advice, things turned out just as I suspected:

I started spending more time with birds.

AND WORDS LIKE THESE

Tilled ground the soft heart, and words
like these the seeds,

and words like these the water, and
words like these a sun.

Beneath the surface of this game, behind
the veil, all is working on your behalf.

Surely then you will rise up and embrace
what will make you most happy.

FREEDOM FROM THE SHACKLE

Once in mid-reach I inquired of my hand,

"Friend, what moves you in that direction?
What hope do you expect to fulfill?"

And an answer came to mind for my hand
has never really talked.

A voice I heard within said, "It is freedom
from the shackle that is the root of all
desire."

It is freedom from the shackle that is the
root of all desire.

APRIL 16

TELL ME OF ANOTHER WORLD

"Tell me of another world," the broken heart
says, "one where love is never sad it loved,
and the word sorry never comes to mind."

"Show me dear God, that anything I have ever
wept for will return, will reside, in my arms."

WHY SAADI SITS ALONE

Your destiny is winding toward the Perfect.

Someday you will be like Saadi,* who sits
alone in wonder,

unable to part from the Darling One, from
the Complete, each of us is becoming.

---

* Saadi Shirazi, Sheikh Mosleh al-Din (c. 1184–1283), better known as Saadi, was
one of the major Persian poets of the medieval period. His still very popular work is
recognized not only for the quality of his writing but also for the depth of his social
thought. A famous poem of his is displayed in the United Nations building in New
York. President Obama brought world-wide attention to that poem in 2009, when
he recited it for the commemoration of Nowruz, the Persian New Year. Emerson
translated some of Saadi's work. And Hafiz considered Saadi a hero—and teacher—
as he was growing up. Hafiz was born nearly 40 years after Saadi died. Their tomb-
shrines, both in Shiraz, are considered the *jewels* of that city.

IN CASE THINGS REALLY GOT HOT

She said I could touch her all I wanted,
a beautiful woman I met.

That inspired me to develop my spirit
body more,

which was less intimidated by time and
space, and had a lot more stamina too . . .
in case things really got hot!

I thought she would have acted more
surprised and delighted when I finally
kissed her with all my passion,

but the moon was more poised than I
knew.

BRINGS LIFE TO A FIELD

It is not possible to complete yourself
without sorrow.

Sorrow is a vital ingredient that shapes
the heart and enriches it.

So endure sadness the best you can
when its season comes.

That rain that can fall from your eye
brings life to a field,

and on other days when you laugh,
a sun takes birth in a sky you will
someday know.

See how all the elements are inside of
you.

See how your soul is a sire of light.

BUT WHAT CAN DIE?

The earth is a host that murders its guests.
But what can die?

All dying just removes more of the husk
over the soul's vision.

All dying thins the veil over a wondrous
world within.

WRITTEN ON THE GATE OF HEAVEN

It is written on the gate of heaven:

Nothing in existence is more powerful than destiny.

And destiny brought you here, to this page, which is part of your ticket—as all things

are—to return to God.

APRIL 22

A REAL BAD DEAL

One who weds for a dowry, or fame, or land
may be lucky if they then find an angel

sleeping next to them at night. Otherwise,
it is usually a real bad deal.

UNTIL NOW I HAD NOT KNOWN

Until now I had not known, but henceforth
will never forget,

The Beloved and each moment are one.

The Beloved and each moment are one.

A CHILD'S MERE PENCIL SKETCH

A child's mere pencil sketch is every religion's
best description of God.

Who then will ever take issue or argue over
such a naïve and innocent portrait?

Surely the intelligent, compassionate, and wise
would not bother with such.

And who with a living heart would not encourage
a child's art in hopes that someday,

someday a great truth and work might be gifted
to our world through their soul's strength, insights
and talents,

and liberate and unite the spheres within a body,
for inherent in true art is emancipation.

And do you have worlds within your self? Indeed.
The night sky a microcosm of you.

The oil in the lamp the sun burns comes from
forests you once were, from rich deposits you left.

TREMENDOUSLY MORE TRUE

She had a dream that told her she was going to pass from this world.

And on the day before, she still felt well, but believed these were her last hours, and come morning friends would be looking at her as she lay still, no longer breathing.

She went into her garden as she always had before dark and spoke to the plants as she would.

Never more beautiful did the world look, never more a part of everything she now knew she was.

An assurance, some absolute certainty opened up in her and she knew any mortal identifications one could have were such a small part of something tremendously more true . . . that awaited our knowing.

Her whole life she saw was like a slipper, often too tight, she had worn for a long day, and did not now mind at all taking it off.

She lay down that night, then merged into a brilliant Sky—someone could call God, she found her soul had always, had always been holding in its hand.

OR TOSS THE RASCALS OUT

Who would want to live with some crickets in
your room carousing loudly all night?

That is to say, either befriend all your thoughts,
party with them the best you can . . . or toss
the rascals out.

YOUR SCENT I KNOW

The ferry to any shore, to any land, to
any realm, it is the wine cup, the heart.

An unseen vessel it is though to most,
love, but so capable of travel, via a prayer
or a soul's deep wish.

And your spirit's arms, they can reach
out and really touch anything you want
to hold.

It should be that way, and it is. For you,
dear, all within time, are right before me.
Your scent I know; your ways I shape.

COAX YOUR MIND

Who can look each day at a beautiful landscape
in the distance and not at some point want to
explore it?

Who can look out at the ocean every morning
and never venture beyond your common horizon

when a boat I am offering to you, and even willing
to do most of the paddling?

It is good if something gnaws at your innards
until you come to real terms with your potential.

God, like a flea, may bite you somewhere to get
your focus to shift.

The Holy, like a good poem, may enter you and
coax your mind . . . to wade out to more
interesting internal space.

BEYOND ANY SILENCE YOU HAVE HEARD

Different trees grow various heights and then
perish and evolve into another species.

They reach their limbs—their souls—a little
deeper into incandescence's well

and then tell the world by their marvelous
appearance *what that life is like.*

Yes, try to do that before you depart this
wondrous place we are visiting;

bring us some good tidings of silence beyond
any silence you have already heard.

RECOGNITION

The word spread about something her eyes
began to whisper, and many gathered to receive
her great gifts when her gaze turned their way.

And it did, for she looked upon all who came
close to her as if she were seeing God. It was
hard to believe the welcome she gave, but I
guess that was natural, with her really knowing
you.

What the sun in the sky can do for the earth,
give it life as it does,

so can the eye bestow an equal grace to the heart
when its vision naturally caresses a face out of
recognition.

Who then does not know a moment of happiness?
And more than that . . . then dance in some way,
because of gratitude.

APRIL 3 1 [*]

WITH ALL THOSE OTHER DOGS HOWLING

Once I was asked, "Hafiz, why do you write poetry?"

To which I quickly responded,

"With all those other dogs howling, I thought I might
as well

j
o
i
n

i
n
!"

---

* A Hafiz-Emerson-Ladinsky bonus poem, just in case there ever is an . . . *April 31.*

— 133 —

MAY

WE ARE LIKE LUTES

We are like lutes once held by God.
Being away from His warm body
fully explains our constant yearning.

MAKING THE ROUNDS AND CAUSING TROUBLE

The words *renounce* and *discipline* were making
the rounds and causing trouble, as some
might expect.

Some newlyweds came to me to discuss the
threat this posed.

They looked at me with serious faces and
sincerely asked,

*Does God want us to renounce the sweet pleasures
our bodies and the earth may give?*

And I replied, *Do what most enables you to fly,
and brings a feeling to the heart that makes you
glad to be alive.*

My guests then said, *Is it really that simple?*

And I said, *Why not?*

RAVE-WORTHY

What is true enlightenment? It is knowing
everything is *rave-worthy*,

but having the balance, the discernment, to
withhold your applause at times, when there are

young souls near . . . or people trying *to sleep*.

GOD, DEPENDENT ON US

Try and stay with me on this one: After being
so connected to the well where all is drawn,

after absorbing God through a refulgent,
pulsating chord at will as easily as most breathe,

curled there—buoyant and surrounded in a
warm sea, knowing your kingdom is light,

yes, having the Infinite rush through your veins
at your merest of commands,

what bravery dear, what strength it takes to
sometimes not openly scream

about such a stupendous loss, even though,
if you listen, all the birds' songs promise—

it is temporary, only temporary . . . God not
being connected to us in a profound intimacy.

You and God are dependent on each other's
being for life.

What else would you like to know today . . . if
that is not enough?

THE HEAVY ARTILLERY

Sound said to me, "I want to be holy." And
I replied, "Dear, what is the problem? You
already are."

Then sound quipped back, "What do you
mean?"

"Well, the wind speaks, does it not? And what
about the refrain of geese? And what of the moo
and the baa and the rooster at dawn,

and the chorus from the sea and the rain, and
the thunder? Is not all a part of God, thus
sacred?

I think He has surrounded us; we better give
up, or He might bring out the heavy

artillery . . . like just outright lifting His skirt
everywhere. Think of the all the sweet madness
that would cause."

INGREDIENTS FROM ALL THOUGHT

There is still a part of you that moves on all fours,
wheels now instead of hooves.

One wheel from the East, one wheel from the West, a
representative of the North, a delegate from the South—
do you know them? They are now a part of your every hour.

I know I am being cryptic. Now I will be more plain.

Ingredients from all thought and realms, and time—
past, present and future—are in you. A few words from
each of the great prophets brought to mind every day
would help all you planted reach its potential, and will
help distill your extraordinary worth.

Reveal yourself to us so that the cries of darkness no longer
disturb any you love. Become that, which the unlit wick
goes to for light.

Heaven guards our souls because they are so precious.
A brightness we can give even God needs. If this was not
true why would He ever bow to us? And that He has, I know.
I have seen His profound humility.

Service to others will help you become deaf to a voice
inside of you that does not believe in happiness. And while
you are at it, remembering things . . . find four poets you
like and imbibe their words into your repertoire.

Then, if you are ever in a jam, there are pawn shops I
know about, where you could cash them in.

A HARD DECREE

Last night God posted on the tavern wall a
hard decree for all of love's inmates which
read:

If your heart can not find a joyful work,
then the jaws of this world will probably
grab hold of your—sweet ass.

MAY 8

ALL SHAPE WOULD COLLAPSE

How many times a paw touched the earth today
I know. I watched and counted them and almost
lost my mind in ecstasy.

The body of everything I became, and now AM, when
God and I smooched so deeply one night. What did you
think might happen then? What is union all about
. . . with the Omnipresent?

Anything's hunt for food I know, I share. Your breathing
draws me in and out. All beings' joys and fears I share.

Something we call God I move with. The holy spirit
is my twin.

Without me all shape would collapse. It is true
I hold you up. Existence's cane is my love.

If I were summoned to a court and accused of being
deluded,

I could supply all the evidence needed to show . . .
all I say is not false.

THAT CUTE HEBREW

Why complain about life if you are looking
for good fish

and have followed some idiot into the middle
of the copper market and then he left you
there . . . stunned and confused.

The above says a lot. It implies at some point
you might actually have to start . . . *thinking*.

Uh-oh.

Yes, uh-oh. And you better get ready. For
evolution at some point will demand it,

that your brain utilize more of its talents and
operate on more of its cylinders—the way
Albert's did.

Einstein, I am talking about. Remember him?
That cute Hebrew with wild hair.

WHEN THE WIND TAKES A TREE IN ITS ARMS

Three-quarters of the world dances all night,
the waves moving as they do on the seas.

And when the wind takes a tree in its arms,
what happens then?

The green branches of the earth may seem to
reach out to touch us if we near them in a forest,
a meadow, a field.

Does not all sway to a rhythm that began long
before we stood upright?

We are in the mountain's home, just guests.
Guests of the sky, the streams, the giving soil
we nurse from.

Would not you be happier following their
example—bowing in unseen ways, then rising
up?

FOR A SINGLE TEAR

I know of beauty that no one has ever
known.

But how could that be possible when I
may seem so new in infinite time?

It is because God belongs to only you!
Did you hear that? Did you hear what
Hafiz just said?

God belongs to only you! That is the only
reasonable payment for a single tear.

ENDURING THE ABSURD

Such a dignity can come to us enduring
the absurd with forbearance and humor.

Elegant becomes the countenance of one
who exemplifies patience.

SIGH AND GIGGLE

When was the last time you wallowed in
contentment,

maybe lay in bed for two days just making
your lover sigh and giggle, and she

and you talked silliness for hours and
joked at the sweet insignificance of most
all stuff?

Cuddle up with the stars more. You will be
able to do that

if you can start treating every human being
as a sacred cow,

and keep a few of my poems handy.

MOVE ON TO YOUR GLORY

What can you see of existence's attempt to honor
you, when you keep turning back to a time
where some *event you seemed to take part in* may
cause you to lower your head, and whisper
again . . . I am sorry?

We are waiting for you to arrive at your own
coronation, but you really can't accept the crown
with any regrets in your past. Where does
that then leave you . . . in line for the throne?

What can you see of every object's attempt
to pay homage to you, because of your divine
lineage, if you are stuck in any kind of
confessional?

All happenings needed to be; accept that, my
dear. Ask for any forgiveness one more time
if you must,

ask for forgiveness one more time if you must,
then move on to your glory and sublime reign.

SPARE THE WORLD YOUR GOOD IDEAS

"Spare the world your ideas of good until you
know all is good," my teacher once said to me.

*Spare the world your ideas of right, until you know
that all is holy.*

THE EXTRAORDINARY INFLUENCE
YOU CAN YIELD

At some point one's prayers will become
so powerful that they can shake a full tree
in an orchard in heaven and fruit will roll
through the streets in this world.

But, dear, until you can do that, maybe
apprentice yourself to someone who can,
and they will help your destiny achieve the
height of the extraordinary influence you
can yield.

WHO WANTS THOSE?

I am at a juncture now where I never have to
be serious again.

If I act that way—sober and concerned about
something . . . it is just a charade.

For people who are serious, well, let's face it . . .
they seem to have lots of problems.

And who wants those?

I LIKE MUSICIANS

Wise the beggar or the thief who can get a coin
from my purse, for it will multiply, it could turn
into emerald worlds.

But what you get from me needs to be held and
not quickly spent. Some kind of incubation is
required.

How can you do that? If you slow your mind
down and keep your aim steady on the present
a heat in your gaze will occur,

something you want to see that was hiding
in the invisible will begin to step forward,
and grow.

Instead of stealing from me, you should know:
I like musicians, and will offer freely to their hat.

HIDDEN

Even the shadow of God is brilliant, so brilliant,
so much so even God has trouble looking at
Himself as that . . . unless He is more disguised,
hidden in illusion, hidden as He can be, in us.

ASKING FOR THE HAND OF MARRIAGE

When someone becomes quiet in this world,
really quiet, those who aren't may turn to
them, even from behind a wall or from a great
distance.

It is like a touch they, the unstill, wanted . . .
a touch that can come from the invisible, come
from an intimate region of the benevolent spirit
in someone in true peace.

Unknown to most, one asks for the hand of
marriage wherever their gaze falls.

I have to stop myself here; sometimes I just
cannot help but to cheer something that
has never quite been put in words before, as
that last line . . . about a "marriage" we always
seek.

That is all I can say now. If there is something
in your mind obstructing your vision, let
someone who can see . . . read all this to you.

The sunflower's heart is not detectable to most,
but you know what it does. It so gladly turns,
offering its body toward its lover—the sun
all day long.

FROM THE MOMENT OF CREATION

From the moment of creation lovers were
assigned the greatest tasks, and became the
most sought after,

and scored the best seats at the finest events,
and won the best vacations from this world.

Vacations? Yes, "vacations" from all we are
not, that can then leave one . . . illumined.

INHABITANTS ON OTHER PLANETS

I am wondering if someone slipped something
in my tea about an hour ago? I feel like I am
on some mind-altering drug. And everything is
telling me jokes.

You know it is not beyond God to take pity on
many down here. He might just surprise you
someday and grind a few million tons of opium
into a fine dust

and then sprinkle it over your house so that
you stop complaining.

You might have to shovel your way out, as if a
big snow came along, smoking it—breathing it
in all the time as it were.

Maybe God does that routinely for inhabitants
on other planets who don't take politics and
gender so seriously . . . or something.

DISTANCE YIELDS

It knew it had no chance. Distance yielded.

Like two opponents meeting and one seeing
it was easily ten times more powerful than
the other,

so the greater warrior just turned and walked
away, but a spear was thrown into its back,
but that was really nothing; it would be pulled
out and laid aside, and even bowed to.

My love has become like that: Ten times the
strength of anything that might ever think to
war with me. And any words shaped like arrows,
what are those to someone my size?

Distance yields. I guess there are two ways of
looking at this, aren't there? One is: Something
will grow in your future. And that is true.

And the other way is: All surrender to the alive
heart, and to the eyes that can be always giving.

May I make a request of my friends? Would you
put some of my words into songs?

It doesn't have to be any words here; they can
come from another bin.

EVERYTHING IN YOUR KINGDOM

It can't forsake you, love. For I know everything
in your kingdom will come to *their* senses someday
and gladly serve your wish.

And the kingdom of each mind stretches so far.
Is there anything not in it?

Would not all your moments of grief, their residue,
end at that juncture where the Sun is walking
toward you—and you toward it, and a union is as
certain *as anything ever was.*

Borrow from your inheritance God has left for you,
and from a dowry He establishes for each creature
as soon as they nurse upon Him.

This is the place to utilize gold, where such rampant
poverty exists upon so many faces caused from
hands acting with greed.

In heaven jewels lie around in the streets; people
have discarded them the way a cow might yesterday's
meal from its rear end;

sweepers come by and shovel them up so that one
won't dirty a foot, or slip.

THE SCENT OF LIGHT

Like a great starving beast my body
is quivering, fixed on the scent of light.

THE HEART'S CORONATION

The pawn always sits stunned, chained,
unable to move beneath God's magnificent
power.

It is essential for the heart's coronation
for the pawn to realize

there is nothing but divine movement in
this world.

AS I WAS THINKING OF YOU

As I was thinking of you three squirrels came
by and all *rubbed their tails against me,*

which reaffirmed my general notion of things,
being: that everyone is really on the right track

even if a wheel now and then gets stuck, or even
runs over someone else.

ANOTHER SQUIRREL TALE

With them being all around my house
and even coming in at times,

how could I not have another squirrel
caper to report?

What I wanted to say of them was, that
I think they can give blessings. Surely
they are like little angels nesting in trees,
who like nuts.

I think they might even be able to
foretell winning lottery numbers, or
point out a good person to date, if you
are lonely.

But you have to be kind to them, or
they will never divulge they can talk.

CAMPAIGNING RELIGIONS

As the intelligence of the human race evolves
all the competing—campaigning as it were—
religions will be viewed differently.

One will see they are all basically contestants
in a beauty pageant,

and the religion that can make your own
beauty most known will win your most respect.

MAYBE ONE LIKE A WATER BUFFALO

Your soul could have chosen a different kind
of body, one that was not nearly as fragile,

one maybe like a water buffalo, more suited
to fender benders, lawsuits and corporate fights.

Actually it tried that, your soul, being other
things, but then decided that a form like yours

was the best jumping-off spot, a springboard
you could say,

for your final somersault . . . into the Beyond.

THIS IS THE WAY TO DIE

Your thousand limbs rend my body.
This is the way to die:

Beauty keeps laying its sharp knife
against me.

JUNE

EVERY CITY IS A DULCIMER

There is the rising up from light's embrace
you can see in a summer field or in a child
dancing.

Every city is a dulcimer that plays its chorus
against our ears.

The lid of a pot starts jumping when the
water gets ecstatic over fire.

If I ever don't complete a sentence while
we are together, accept my apologies

and try to understand this sweet, drunk
thought.

Birds initially had no desire to fly; what
really happened was this:

God once sat close to them playing music.
When He left they missed Him so much

their great longing sprouted wings, needing
to search the sky.

Listen, for Hafiz knows, nothing evolves us
like love.

A WHITE GULL HEADING EAST

A sailor lost for days at sea in a boat all alone
spots a white gull heading east at dawn,

and for a moment her sight becomes his.
Things can happen like that; your soul can
enter another—that fully.

Land, land! he cried within, and then even
tasted the earth in a way,

and so felt saved, as one might if one's mouth
touched God and all your hungers disappeared

for a blessed second, which can also occur while
reading a half-decent poem,

so hope you find one somewhere. Don't give up
if this falls short.

WHO WOULD MESS WITH ME NOW?

A magnificent force I have become,
having aligned myself with Truth.

Who would mess with me now?
Only a lucky idiot.

So, go ahead. *Egg my house*, or steal
some fruit from that pear tree in
my backyard.

That would be a good idea, to imbibe
something I have tended, like these
playful words.

THE BED OF THE SICK

God is always there, beside the bed of the sick.
So many times He holds a cup to their mouths
and strokes their head.

If you don't believe me, try picturing that in your
mind, happening to you.

Enact this beautiful scene if ever you feel in need
of the Beloved's presence.

That is what an imagination is for. Can you think
of anything better to do with it? And who is to say
it won't become real . . . somewhere along your
path.

FALLING ON A SOFT MAT

More attentive than any lover or parent
is really God to us, but our gauge of judgment
is impaired by the world's values, and our bodies'
often dominance over our spirit realm.

A young child first learning to walk and very
likely to fall may be allowed to do so by a wise
guardian or teacher

if there is a soft mat beneath its body that will
cushion it from harm.

There is a soft rug you can place around others
it is forgiveness, it is charity.

We are all still learning to walk—and fly—in
ways; kin help each other. And *everything* I am
related to.

ENERGY IN SOUNDS

As many times as a parrot might say any
number of things, will that make them true
for the bird?

So it is with many utterances about spiritual
matters from people; they just may never occur
except in make-believe, which probably won't
pay the rent.

Harness speech; let it become a windmill
that can grind a harvest.

There is a pristine energy in sounds that
come from certain depths that can help split
the atom

if you can control them perfectly, which would
mean your words cease to harm, and always
uplift, or at least comfort.

With the world so ripe for help, this is what
our relationship is at times about—

me increasing your power, so that you can bake
a special wheat, that can feed the various longings
a refined heart can know.

GO SCREW YOURSELF

Like a salesman who once scored at your house,
the mirage keeps sending you offers.

The illusion, being persistent, used to knock at
my door, so I began to shout, *Go screw yourself!*

That helped some, but maya did not finally go
away until I sat for forty days in silence, and
took full control over my life.

Now, just the turning of my head can send out
a wake that shatters any phantom I wish.

A COAT RACK

Let this page be a coat rack you leave something
on.

Something that you will be better off without.
Something that if you no longer carry its weight

you will look less cunning and dangerous, less
inclined to explode.

And you will know more mirth if a thorn in your
mind you let me keep; a pin-cushion my being,
why not, for you?

Then the scent of your love will reach others and
help draw them from their places of hiding,

their shields they won't need anymore to veil, to
hold between our embrace.

The world will be known as more miraculous,
tender, fun and always giving,

and your hands, angel, will then too be able to
carry more of God off, wherever you like to go.

You could set *Him all around* in places that you
wish Him found.

FIND A BETTER JOB

Now that all your worry has proved such an
unlucrative business . . . why not find a better
job?

And while you are at it, scouting about town
and fine tuning your resume, maybe light a
candle in some church.

LITTLE ERECT THINGS FEEL PROUD

I heard that in some monasteries there were
human skulls on the tables where the monks
ate to remind them of their transitoriness,

and that they wore *hair coats* sometimes and
maybe even whipped themselves, and would
even mutilate their bodies if they ever had a
sexual desire.

In the spring God looks happiest it seems,
when it is clear a beautiful force is surely active
on earth—as if the Conductor lifted its baton

and everyone started to cuddle, and fur and
feathers danced against each other's moist *hot
spots.*

Little erect things feel proud, parade about,
and then get stuck here and there. Depression
reaches a low point in the mating season; maybe
we should extend it to being year-round?

But maybe you have tried that? Did it work?
Send us a report.

IF I DID NOT KNOW YOUR NAME

I think it is time for a joke. You tell me one.
I will take it easy here a minute and listen.

What is a mere few years, centuries, or
millenniums between us? I should be able
to follow . . . any contemporary language.

I have entered such a state—that I don't
think will go away—to where I have heard

every word anyone has ever spoken. Past,
present, and future. Why not?

I am on a float trip in the Buddha's mind.
Limits don't exist. All knowledge is there and
not there, simultaneously,

surrounded by a brilliant splendor even I can
still hardly believe is really true.

If I did not know your name, you whose
face is close to what I have written,

I might doubt my own experience, for it is
just so sublime.

HE DIDN'T WANT TO THINK ANYMORE

He didn't want to think anymore, a young
man I heard about, so he traveled far and
checked himself into an ashram, where most
lose IQ points each day and after a while
just babble or keep silent.

Sometimes, though, the monastic life can
do just the opposite: increase the brain
and heart's power. It simply depends on who
one turns the reins of life over to.

My general advice is: Anyone wearing spiritual
robes is potentially lethal; best to consider they
already have two strikes against them . . . and
if they make just one tiny false move—best to
run, or hit them with your bat.

And a word about dead gurus reincarnating.
Most are just that, deadbeats. A lot of very
tricky psycho games can go on with them, in
which your bank account might weep.

BUMP HEADS WITH THE ROOF

"How can I grow and reach my full height?"
a tree once said to me.

And I replied, "Dear, sit quiet for a minute
each day, don't let your branches move,

conserve your energy within and without,
concentrate all your strength on your invisible
wings.

Then a fuel that feeds your actions and
thoughts will help your spirit

to rise and bump heads with the *Roof* over all."

YOUR FIDELITY TO LOVE

Your fidelity to love, that is all you need.
No day will then match your strength.

What was once a fear or problem will see
you coming, and step aside . . . or run.

PRAY TO YOUR HAND

The foundation for insanity is laid, and every
moment it increases as the universe expands.

Too convincing for most everyone is *form* to
then not call it real. And to not then be its
wholehearted servant at times.

Some balance, dear, some delicate discernment
is required between what appears to be and
what really is not.

Let it often come down to this, for the right
equation you need to solve the big dilemma
is just too vast for most.

Yes, let it come down to this, when thoughts
and aspects of the infinite can no longer delight
you:

Pray to your hand that it reveals all the wonder
you will ever need to be satisfied. For it is
there. The divine mystery is in all things.

REMEMBER A SONG YOU KNOW

If you are sad, remember a beautiful song
you know. It is really something living.

It can bring you to the place where it was
created *out of light*, and you can feel that
for a moment.

If you do not wish to sing, if you are feeling
shy or just too low, picture me doing so,
while

sitting at a table with you, with maybe a
drink in our hands . . . toasting

something you would like to clink a cup
with me about, my dear.

THIS IS THE TIME FOR SILENCE

The beauty of the mountain is talked about
most from a distance,

not while one is scaling the summit with
life at risk. That is the time for silence,
one-pointedness,

reflection, and drawing upon all your
skills so you might return from the cloud's
domain

and inspire others to breathe closer to God,
while still human, the way you did.

ONE OF THE DUMBEST THINGS YOU CAN DO

One of the dumbest things you can do is
backbite an animal, or a human being.

Reason is: Besides the fact that an animal
who is feeling grouchy that day might bite
you back . . .

whenever you speak ill of any living creature
something of their shadow might fall on you.

Some unwanted impressions of theirs could
spill on your floor,

and I imagine you are busy enough trying
to keep things tidy.

AN ENTHUSIASM TO EXPRESS DISCOVERY

Some painters were engaged in a passionate
conversation about the *value of art.*

It was an interesting discussion that I listened
to almost an hour without speaking.

Then a young woman turned to me and said,
"Any comments, Hafiz?" And these thoughts
came to mind that I spoke:

*The greatest and most lasting art, the impetus
of it, I feel, always comes from a wanting to help.
A wanting to free, and an enthusiasm to express
discovery.*

*Each soul at some point will begin to feel all is
within it and then attends, as it were, to its own
inner world. That attendance may not result in
anything considered tangible reaching the masses.*

*But the artist also becomes aware of inner spheres
and mingles with them, and then puts those
experiences into what they most care about for the
world to see and touch if the world wants.*

*I know all my poems come from a wanting to give
something useful.*

MORE AWAKE IN DREAMS

Many are more awake, with greater
abilities in dreams, than in the daylight.

I walked through a world last night of
such exquisite intricacies . . . in my sleep
some might say.

But no, it was not really like that. It
was surely as real as any place you ever
visited.

Whatever the hand can shape and make
last . . . the advanced mind can do a
millionfold.

And love, there too while I slept so alert
with perceptions keen and powerful,

did I know you, love, and could more
bear your fire.

In dream, in spirit, are we not closer to
Her likeness?

THE NIGHT ORCHARD

The night orchard is in bloom, the clear sky.
How many people have looked upon her face
and called her by different names?

Still she responds as if there is something so
personal just between you and her.

Does not she even appear to be willing to
become intimate with your ways? Who taught
those sweet manners?

About the heart, what can I say? Complaints
I have known vanished.

It was bound to happen, with all the best
that one might believe of God . . . will come
true. And more.

ABRACADABRA-DOO

A mantra I heard about seemed to work for an eccentric
uncle I had whenever he needed a boost.

That mantra went . . . *Abracadabra-doo.* And sometimes
he would say *Abracadabra-boo!*

Personally, I think it was that *boo* that somehow pulled it
all together and gave it any needed final punch

to chase any unwanted devious spirits away who may have
been siphoning off vital juices.

Just for the record though: I really don't believe in magic
lamps, genies and things like that,

and any three wishes you might ever really want, someone
like me could deliver if you honed your charms enough.

But what the hell, maybe say it a couple of times a year
with gusto . . . *Abracadabra-boo,* or *Abracadabra-doo!*

Consider singing both in some kind of unison, you might
as well with all the other wacky things you have tried.

I WADE OUT INTO OTHER FORMS

It used to come and go as it wanted, it seemed,
love. It left me feeling helpless.

I wondered if there might be some kind of leash
I could slip around its neck to remedy that
situation, cherishing certain emotions as I did.
Not wanting them to wander off.

An idea occurred to me: to hold God accountable
when He said, *In my image I have made you.*

I demanded to see that, I started to picket His
house, to *see* more of myself.

Waves of Him now greet my shore. I wade out
into other forms of myself. And I swim in what
I never thought I could.

Inseparate is any creature or object from Light,
from the Ocean, became my discovery.

PICK THE LOCK

There are so many keys on your ring,
so many fine spiritual sayings you can
recite, and maybe so many pictures of
saints in your house.

But you rarely work hard enough, peer
deep enough, to pick the lock.

You should have stopped reading pages
ago, if not in this book, in another,

and just sat down and done whatever
it took to grab God by the tail and pull
Him from a cave in you.

TO MAKE YOU PERFECT

It helps to see the Goldsmith's kind face
before he rolls up his sleeves,

and starts pumping the bellows, and
cleans off his wire brush and other tools,

then eyeing you like he knows how much
this is going to hurt, to make you perfect.

A LATE NIGHT SNACK

I know there are a lot of important things
going on in the world that maybe I should in
some way be attending.

But I was wondering how those pretty spiced
apples, just out of the oven—and in all of their
aromatic glory

will taste for dessert, and then a late night snack.

HOLDS US CAPTIVE

Look at the sweetness of their play, those
lion cubs. Look at part of beauty's beauty,

it holds us captive to what delights.

All those paws in a dancing motion, they
are a blessing to my eye.

It should be like this; all that can open the
heart in heaven . . . can be found on earth.

Love reveals the paradise.

HE BELONGED IN A MORGUE

He looked like he belonged in a morgue
three days ago, an old neighbor of mine.
Then a young woman moved in with him.

They were up till 3:00 a.m. last night
rocking the walls. A week from now he
may look worse off than when this tale
began.

But for the moment I am glad things are
going well. Maybe there are some clues
here to help enliven you?

And in case you have noticed, I know I
have discussed this matter before. It just
seems to keep coming up.

WHEN NO ONE CAN SAY THE RIGHT WORDS

When the body begins to die, and no one can
say the right words,

it is then that a poem may find the courage to
come forth and try to be with you.

So intimate is the experience of death, in some
ways even more so than birth.

All the work you have done for self and family
and maybe even the world, whatever labor it
was, it should be known—it was really astounding.

And what you did just standing in an hour . . .
against all time,

herculean your efforts, your every movement;
that is true. You can rest now, dear. Rest.

Turn into what you were before you came. That
will be offered before you leave us.

The miraculous will not end. Even sweeter you
will smile.

And if you wish, a cheek you cherished, you will
soon touch again.

WHEN ALL IS STILL

And then, all the *and then*s ceased.
Nothing remains *to be done* in the

order of time, when all is still. In the
profound quiet, the immaculate comes
into view. God disrobes.

JULY

MOSES AND THE PINUP GIRL

Who is to say that Moses was not sweet on a
local pinup girl, and pinup boy,

and when Moses was not acting like a religious
wild man

they often appeared as a damn cute

t
h
r
e
e
s
o
m
e
?

THE COURAGEOUS DIRTY WORK

I am glad someone thinks they *are real,*
real enough that they respond to names,
real enough to show up for work on time
and pay their bills.

For what would happen to the world if
there weren't courageous people like that
around,

willing to do the dirty work . . . *of thinking*
they exist?

NESTS IN YOUR PALM

What makes the wings return in the spring,
I know all about.

And what makes them leave again before the
snow weighs down their need for flight? That
feeling too I am very familiar with.

Look at your own migration from spirit to
form and back, so many times.

What is there to learn before you can retire
and cease such an arduous journey?

Even His son was here to sweat and fast, and
to work with his hands, and draw from a well
and quench the thirst of myriad shapes.

Until you discover heaven nests in your palm,
you will keep traveling in widening circles,

in exploration from spirit to form, until there
is that deep *Ahhh* inside, and then nowhere
else you will want to go.

Students then might gather, wanting to imbibe
your ways.

WHEN THE MEADOWS ON THE BODY
TURN GRAY

When the meadows on the body begin to turn
gray, let your eye soften toward yourself, and those
who are close.

Let anyone, anything, *inside* who has driven you,
let them retire or move at an easier pace.

And where you were once firm, and might have
even said to someone, *feel my muscle,* or admired it
yourself,

yes, now look at the way you have become, or will
someday if you live as long as you may want.

Many do all they can to not have to face the candle
going out.

The wonder of my body aging, dying, is finding
another flame within, a holy eternal

sphere, that will never go out and is more beautiful
than all the form you have known—put together.

When the fields on the body begin to turn gray
let your hand's touch upon all, soften.

WHO LAUGHS THE MOST

Who laughs the most knows the most,
if that laughter is sincere.

UNTIL THEY BECOME A SKY AGAIN

The peace, it is there; it grows from her soil.
A few feet beneath her surface, all is always
perfectly calm.

What does she know of any storms then? What
does she hear of any cries of this world, or is
in any way startled by fear?

Once in a while something stirs a thirst she
had forgotten about;

a divine rain falls on her hills and settles in a
beautiful valley;

there, life's companion, water, gently reaches
down and touches, awakens her heart.

She begins to reach up with all her strength,
feeling a glorious destiny awaits,

and she keeps stretching out her arms until
they become a sky again and all that is
luminous in it.

Her love shelters then from all angles, above,
below . . . and to our sides.

Yes, it shelters us, any heart, like an earth,
that knows God.

The peace is always there, just beneath a
particle of our surface.

THE MIRACLE OF DARKNESS

Now, with illuminating spheres appearing
wherever I turn and something even greater,

tell me God, more of your miracle of darkness
I can see in other lives.

I once cried for what was not in my hand,
not knowing it was there.

Finally you pointed out my fantastic
misconception and corrected it.

Darkness, would be a miracle to me now,
my head having become pure fire.

THE TRUTH IS, I HAVE BEEN COVERING YOUR BUTT

The truth is, I have been covering your butt,
God, for quite a while now in various ways

by not telling the world how you really are
behind that eloquent pose most holy books
are sporting of you.

This morning, though, it occurred to me
to just speak my mind, to just be forthright,

and get all my complaints out there in the
open so that we might have some kind of
public forum if you felt brave enough.

Are you ready? Okay then!

Here is one of my major gripes: Why would
anyone ever have to do anything to be let
back into *their own house,*

especially if it were cold outside and they
were shivering

and they were hungry too, and there was
lots of fresh warm food inside?

Another way of putting that is, if someone
were walking in front of me and

unknowingly dropped something precious,
something of extraordinary value,

Continued on July 9th

THE TRUTH IS, I HAVE BEEN COVERING
YOUR BUTT (2)

What kind of person would I be if I did not run
as quickly as I could and pick that up

and use all my strength to protect and safeguard
it until I could return it?

Return it, if possible, without the person
having a moment, a moment of worry or

pain with the thought of it being lost.

I have fallen out of my own pocket. My own
pocket being you, Beloved.

Millions like me cry at night because something
is so deeply amiss.

The agony of separation you have caused us
to endure.

You follow our every step, dear God; you saw
what happened to us,

severed in a way from the infinite soul we became
when we lost the knowledge you, my Lord, have.

Why, why, why? Why, why, why are you not
running toward us with all your might

returning to us our glory, our freedom—
which is beyond dispute . . . our divine right?

Continued on July 10th

THE TRUTH IS, I HAVE BEEN COVERING YOUR BUTT (3)

I will tell you something about shame, God,
if you want to know.

You are the only one who should ever feel
that way, never us,

for you have stepped over a holy infant all
alone, dying in the cold.

I could go on tearing you apart, as I should,
but now I will give you a chance to speak,
after this final thought:

We should stop making excuses for you, my
strange Friend,

for how dare you make us beg for what you
say is ours?

No wonder you so rarely show your face,
acting as you do.

Still, is not all perfect, since all is in you? And
what may appear, will that not in *just a moment
change,* if you want.

Look, my love, I am back to covering your hiney
again. What to say. Guess a friend does that.

Continued from July 9th

WHERE I ONCE SANG

It gently faded, all I once believed in. But
I am glad there is a world that seems to go
on where I once sang.

All I ever knew is still a part of me, and
will be forever.

All I ever knew is like a little mouse living
in a tiny hole in a palace I have become.

Since God gave me the key to Myself, I
know the movements of every limb, fin and
leaf. I could tell you how many hairs exist
on every creature on earth.

Sometimes it, that sweet little rodent, comes
out and we look at each other,

and I even talk to that wondrous world
where I once lived, as I am doing right now.

IT IS A HOLY WOMAN & A TEMPLE

It is a holy man, a good poem, and a holy
woman; and a temple and a mosque and a
shrine.

Have you not been looking for a companion
like that? For a place of such great refuge,

where time asks nothing of you, where you
can come and go as you please, where you
basically control all the rules because your
heart knows best.

And don't have to give up any pleasures that
might still be working, adding color to your
cheeks.

There is nothing you touch that you hope
won't fit into a puzzle you are seriously
working on.

I know how the eye works, what its primary
impetus and desire is: to lay its gaze upon the
beautiful, and for beauty to wink back.

The eye, like every part of you, is governed by
your great and continual primal instinctive need
to feel whole and able. Able to work and learn
and give and play—and love and love. Who
would deny that?

It is a holy woman, a decent poem, and a holy
man; and a temple and a mosque and a shrine.

Carry any relics from my words that you can.

THE ROOT OF THE ROSE

In this cup I am drinking from, I can see *the Face behind every face,*

A well now, where creation has been drawn, I am. How can a jug being carried on the top of my head contain everything?

A galaxy can appear in the reflection of a small clear pool.

Right where the moon may appear smiling at you from a body of still water . . . a fish might leap out

and swallow that orb whole, and who is to say, maybe then lay it at your feet?

Within an arm's reach is all I desire, so I am never in want.

The root of the Rose I have become, from loving the way I did.

THREW THEM OUT OF WHACK

Sometimes when visitors come and words
have done what they can, I say,

*There is a lute in the room where I rest. Go
there, please, and fetch that, for I am having
trouble walking these days.*

*I will play you a tune that came to me last
night when I was bowed in prayer,*

*for I noticed this morning when I hummed it
some angels with hangovers gathered near
and they felt better.*

*It is not that they were drinking things we
do; it is that they stepped into the minds*

*of some humans for a while, and that really
threw them out of whack.*

EASIER TO CUDDLE WITH

Sometimes I feel as if I am involved with the
extraordinary;

that something of my efforts—and their
results—are a great triumph, for both of us;

that something I have labored with added
to a bridge, we can cross to see the Beloved
more as He is: *Damn easier to cuddle with.*
And always inviting.

What a great athlete might feel in a moment
of joy and wonder, in accomplishing the
nearly impossible, I have known that—and
much more.

You are extraordinary to my eye, everything
about anyone.

Others too can see you as I do, but rarely
do they have an interest in the pen.

I am telling you the truth. It is difficult to
bear your splendor.

How I just don't explode and vanish—pop
from ecstasy, I don't know?

This is just another astonishing event, another
one of those divine *mysteries* . . . we can hear
about, and is worthy of the *evening news.*

THAT BELIEVE IN GRAVITY

The wind and I could come by and carry
you the last part of your journey, if you
became light enough,

by just letting go of a few more things you
are clinging to . . . that still believe in
gravity.

I HAVE WINCED AT THE PROSPECT

I have winced at the prospect of reading a
long poem. Even my own.

That happened the other day when I found
one hiding behind the couch, and I braved
exploring *its terrain.*

If that could happen to me, I thought,
*oh my goodness, what about you coming across
drunken ramblings?*

For any unpleasant twitches and pain I have
caused you, apologies extended.

HEAVEN IS JEALOUS

There are moments in moist love when heaven
is jealous of what we on earth can do.

And there are gods who would trade their lives
to have a heart that can know human pain,

because our sufferings will allow us to become
greater than any world or deity.

STILL HE LIFTS THE MALLET

Still he lifts the mallet, still he may
draw the sword, still he might speak
out for a cause he knows is right.

And prayer the heart may continue,
and even cry. For all is contained in
the perfect woman, and in the perfect
man.

THERE WOULD BE FEWER BIRD SONGS

There would be fewer bird songs if our
perceptions were greater, less calling out in
need, less offering praise; no more *seeking noises*.

Probably more than half the tunes, the
sounds you make, could retire when one's
Beloved is discovered within an easy reach.

If your left hand began to publicly thank your
right for helping it with a task, or bringing about
some comfort to you or family, that would be a
sign you needed professional help.

Someday, for doing meditation, prayer or yoga
in a crowd they might just cart you off to the nut
house. I will come visit you though, and help you
learn about being invisible, and silent.

We were torn from the throne where we sat, all
we do is a trying to restore ourselves. There are
people like Attar* in this world who carry a
thousand crowns in each pocket wanting to bless,
sanction, our many stages, stations, on the path.

---

* Muhammad Attar was Hafiz's teacher and master. Hafiz was a young man of
about 20 when they met. It is believed he spent about 40 years with Attar, often
seeing him every day. Attar is recognized today, by some of the greatest spirituality
authorities, to have been a Perfect Master.

WOULD IT NOT BE?

Many times I have been asked, *What is it like to know the Truth?*

And my answers have varied depending on who posed the question, but this one I have never quite said before,

and it is, *To know the Truth is to be able to enjoy deeply anything, anything that can happen in this world.*

For the one who knows the Truth knows all is perfect. But sometimes it is best I pretend as if it is not. Some words come to mind about this, they are:

There are wings that can applaud even the madness but to it never add one's own precious touch.

The seer can see any event as if it were *the only* event that has ever happened in creation, *or will happen,*

thus all appears miraculous, miraculous. Would it then not?

MECCA AND I BUMP HEADS

There are protective layers, veils between you
and God's effulgence,

otherwise your face would appear singed,
scarred from ecstasy as mine.

Such honorable wounds though, are bound to
someday be yours.

If you looked close you would see my eyes
are always folded in way, like hands praying.

The sun and the moon are my knees at hours,
and the sky, the sky a prayer mat.

Mecca and I bow to each other and bump our
heads, that is how close we are.

The ocean asks me to baptize it, when I walk
along its body. And how can I resist?

I stopped exaggerating a couple years ago,
when God and I did wed.

IF GOD INVITED YOU TO A PARTY

If God invited you to a party and said,

"Everyone in the ballroom tonight will
be my special guest,"

how would you then treat them when
you arrived? Indeed, indeed!

And Hafiz knows there is no one in this
world who is not standing upon His

jeweled dance floor.

HOW DOES IT FEEL TO BE A HEART?

Once a young woman said to me, "How
does it feel to be a man?"

And I replied, "My dear, I am not so sure."
Then she said, "Well, aren't you a man?"

And this time I responded, "I view gender
as a beautiful animal that people often take

for a walk on a leash and might enter into
some odd contest . . . in hopes of winning a
strange prize."

My dear, a better question for Hafiz would
have been, "How does it feel to be a heart?"

For all I know is love, and I now find my
heart infinite, and everywhere.

SWEET, THREATENING SHOUTS

Throw away all your begging bowls at
God's door,

for I have heard the Beloved prefers
sweet, threatening shouts, something

on the order of, "Hey, Beloved, my soul
is a raging volcano of love for you!

You better start kissing me—*or else!*"

THE WORLD MORE BEARABLE

Knowing how she can benefit us, beauty
sometimes acts like a hooker.

Because she knows if we spend an hour with
her we will be better off.

And beauty is right, she is clever. When has
looking at the graciousness in nature or in art,
or hearing some moving music

not softened your face, made your touch
more wanted, your voice more rich and alive,

and the world more bearable. And the sweet
taste of hope yours and able to impart.

YOUR SIGHT EMBRACING ALL

I sometimes watch the movement in an egg,
in a nest on a cliff no one has ever neared,
in a world that has not even been named.

The purity of all, its wonder, *and your sight
embracing everything*, how could that ever be?
Some kind of real omniscience?

You will never be able to work that extraordinary
piece of the puzzle into your ken

believing so strongly in—and even being such
an advocate at times . . . of right and wrong, as
you probably are.

WHAT ELSE CAN I DO FOR YOU?

"What else can I do for you," the sky said,
and added, "now that I have taken off all
my clothes?"

There are some lines of value to *contemplate,*
the above, and even worthy—to my keen
estimation—*of writing home to mom about.*

WE ADD TO OURSELVES OR DETRACT

Every time you open your mouth and let a sound
out, you alert the prey. And who is not hunting
because of some hunger?

What you seek may run in different ways. Or
people you know may begin to snarl within when
they see you coming.

We add to ourselves or detract whenever we speak.
Our words turn into an entity and a magnetic field
someone has to reckon with.

I have found it is best to be on good terms with as
much as one can—controlling the notes from the
flute, from the body, that can rise.

Yes, we add to ourselves or detract, in some ways,
with each movement. I have increased my worth
so much, a treasury I have become, I hope you loot.

A CROWBAR

I left a crowbar in some of these poems.
You can have it.

It came in handy for breaking into His
house, before I found out . . . I owned

the joint.

HAPHAZARD BRILLIANT THOUGHTS

There are not many teachers in this world who can
give you as much enlightenment in one year --

as sitting all alone for three days in your closet would
do. That means no leaving,

so better get a friend to help with a few sandwiches
and the chamber pot if you ever give it a try.

And no alcohol in there or illegal drugs, books, or pens
and paper to write down any brilliant thoughts that
might haphazardly wander through your head.

Think non-attachment. Aim high for a 360 degree
detox. Stop musing for a while . . . *you are* who you
aren't.

This 72 hour retreat though, is not recommended if
your emotional state has ever been under any kind of
professional surveillance!

Dear ones, don't let Hafiz fool you. There is usually,
like right now, a ruby buried in what I say. Grab it,
and don't let go . . . till your horizons expand.

AUGUST

TWO GIANT FAT PEOPLE

God and I have become like two giant
fat people living in a tiny boat;

we keep bumping into each other and

l
a
u
g
h
i
n
g
.

BARELY ONE YOU WISH TO HARM

There are only so many people you can
carry in your small boat before their
weight sinks you.

A hundred you can carry whom you love.
But barely one you wish to harm.

SOFTER THAN A MOUTH

So tender the eye's true vision, softer
than a mouth, so when any look at
me . . . as gentle as heaven I am seen.

For not a word is heard in the place
where benevolence reigns. Not a word
that does not lift a wing.

YOU BETTER RETHINK THIS

In case you forget, pain is there to help with
your decisions.

Like if you pick up a pot that is too hot, it
will burn you; that quick, sharp sting arrives
in a second, saying . . . *you made a mistake,*
you better rethink this.

And if you were walking in a jungle and a
roar came from some dense brush up ahead,
would you then walk straight into that unless
you were a giant looking to have some fun . . .
and duke it out with some beast for a little
morning exercise?

It is all around and built into our senses,
warnings about things we just should not do.
Why?

Because the dance floor wants to be polished
with your feet moving on it at night.

How will you do that sitting at home nursing
wounds or feeling depressed?

WISHING YOU WERE HERE

Those kisses you sent, I found them wandering around the house. They were acting a little lost, not knowing exactly where I was.

I was busy upstairs. But now we are all having tea and talking about you, and wishing you were here.

And they imparted all you intended. They did well.

One more thing: I have seen you at your best and at your worst; still you are always welcome near me.

A BLUE RIBBON REAR END

It would be easy to change the world. It could
happen in a couple of days,

if everyone with a *blue ribbon rear end* agreed
to not let any rich or powerful person touch it!

Touch it—unless all those gilded weirdos made
some serious promises to revamp their strange
ways.

Think of all the leverage that we could then
have; we could begin to sway major elections,

we could get seats on corporate boards, we could
take over the stock market and the Vatican too,
I bet. Hmmmm!

Yes, it is bound to work, with promiscuity and
lust's charms having most in a *full nelson.**

---

* *full nelson:* A wrestling hold that is hard to get free of.

WELL NOW

Well now. What else could I say but *well now*
and *hmmmm* again! Seeing all the commotion
that last poem might cause.

Especially since it is true! And we could do it . . .
rule the universe for the betterment of the many.

So, next time that *queen* starts eyeing my behind,
I will just say straight out . . . *No way buddy, get
lost.*

IF YOU JUST UNTIE THE SUN

All your problems can be solved. All your problems can be solved, if you just untie that sun that somehow got leashed on a pole in you.

— 244 —

IF WHAT YOU SAY BECOMES MEMORABLE

Most that is said is really like a distant echo.
Few minds are strong enough,

free enough of prejudice and arrogance for
original thought to want to pass through.

The body is like a vase, a bell that can chime.
It does so to varying degrees in response to
every experience and feeling.

The value of *vases* can differ, as you know,
quite a bit.

How does heaven assign worth to our sounds?
It comes down to this:

If what you say or do becomes memorable to
another in times of need,

an ally are you then considered by the gods.

WHO COULD READ ALL THIS?

To God, there is never a question of giving or not giving . . . Her mercy.

And yes, let's call God a *Her* sometimes to balance out all that male testosterone that took over the world's holy books;

they look gender-biased to me. I think we should sue someone right now . . . before it gets too late and some statute of limitations expires.

God's mercy is a natural reflex; moreover it is just there. It is like the water in a lake—a fish should never ask permission to drink or be alive in.

As much thought as a fish would give to any needed divine sanction to move his fins or piddle in the Ocean, so is there a proportionate suffering meant to correct any screwed up notions you harbor about Truth.

I don't want to explain this; if your teacher really knows anything, she can.

Mercy and Grace are just there; they are attributes of light, they want nothing but to be.

God wants nothing in return for your existence. What madness to ever think you owe Him/Her/It anything.

Gosh, who could read all of this? But maybe it is a *perspicuous move*.

SOCIALIZE A BIT

Shortly after my rooster crowed a favorite tune of his, a lizard appeared on a rock, close to where I was sitting, and practiced some new jokes.

Then a rabbit popped out of her hole and we discussed some essential matters, till an old dog, another pal of mine, came by.

Some birds that knew I was an easy mark gathered for their breakfast of seeds & crumbs.

The wind then whispered something in code, and I started clapping.

As lively as things can get around me—and all the friends I have, truth is:

I live in a dimension where there is only the Rose. Not a trace of me.

But I can step from that sublime state and socialize a bit.

HOW ETERNITY COULD BE ENDURED

You must have seen yourself by now—I mean
the real Self. It must have at least passed close
by one day, maybe even stepped on your toes.
Or dragged you somewhere.

That Self, upon your seeing it, gave you the idea
of how eternity could be endured, because of a

tremendous enchantment you felt for a grace
emanating from all things, and your soul now
the epicenter. *Your own presence, upon every
throne.*

Such an incandescence you emanated, and so
magnificently sovereign you felt, that rightfully,

rightfully, all your ideas of God would look very
pale if they had the audacity to stand next to
you, when your sight was clear . . . *and all your
power revealed.*

WOMEN IN THEIR TENDER WAY

God listens more to women's prayers than
men's when women are in their tender way.

Because often they have achieved with the
blessings of earth

what a man can rarely do on his own: bring
empathy, sensitivity and kindness into the heart
and mind,

and make the voice more tender, one's touch
more gentle, one's plea more powerful from it
being so sincere.

It is holy, blood. And all that can come from a
body.

As if it were part of God, everything should be
enshrined.

GIVING THANKS IS DANGEROUS

Giving thanks is dangerous, for inherent in
doing so is to reaffirm duality. And duality
is living on borrowed time.

Thanks to God are most always an admitting,
always a making of a statement that basically

says, "I am glad things are no longer as they
were."

From perfect to perfect we go. From unconscious
divinity to conscious God.

A masterpiece you always were. Anyone who
truly sees would never want you to change,

though the teacher may play the horrific
game of right and wrong

so that you won't kill yourself. Or you won't
dissolve in bliss, until you have given to this
world all you were supposed to; or something
like that.

GEE WHIZ

Gee whiz. Make that a double—*Gee whiz,*

for I bet all the Masters said something like
that . . . quite often

when looking out upon the world—though
I have not yet been able to substantiate
that with enough scholarly data . . .

to mention it with any confidence in an
important lecture I am supposed to give
next week.

THERE IS NO SPOT ON EARTH

There is no spot on earth that ever became
sacred until something danced there; maybe
it was just an atom or two.

Strange now the seriousness I see around
the shrines of perfect saints

whose feet once wept ecstatic tears as they
moved upon the sun they saw beneath our
every step.

There is no place in existence that ever
became sacred until something sang there,

even be it just a molecule. That is enough.
I hear they croon all the time.

DON'T RUN AND WASH YOUR HANDS

Don't run and wash your hands if the Beloved
ever offers something to you.

He knows where they have been, out touching
the holy, via His many forms.

WE HAVE SOME LEVERAGE

Always assume you are on the best of terms
with God, for, dear, I will tell you a truth:
We have some leverage over Him.

How do I know this? It was pretty easy to
figure out with this fine brain.

In short: Each of us is like His only heir.

Spoiled and difficult as we may be, He is
very willing to put up with us until we are
enthroned.

IT IS MY NATURE

It is the nature of this world to share
its burden with you.

And it is my nature to remove it from
your back.

MUHAMMAD'S TWIN

I know the one you are looking for,
I call that man Muhammad's twin.

You once saw him, so now your eyes
are weaving a great net of tenderness

that will one day, one day capture
God.

I know the one you are looking for,
I call that man Muhammad's twin.

LET ME THINK A SECOND

Some great high-wire act the path to
God becomes.

And look at that long pole that is also
needed to balance you, so you don't fall.

And look at that long pole that is also
needed to gain balance, so you don't
fall.

Let me think a second. How about in
part:

doing something that you know will
be good for you,

that you have not yet done. And of
course, humility, and of course kindness.

IN A MANNER I WON'T FORGET

Tell me, love, what I need right now so that
I might sing, and be alive, as my every cell
craves.

Tell me, dear, what I need right now, but
in a manner I won't soon forget.

Then the world began to sway, its hips
invited my arms, its feet placed mine upon
them, that made all my effort easy.

A father's toes lifting a child's in dance caused
God to pull out a drum.

The Beloved belted out a tune, that went,
"Nothing to follow . . . for I will move you.
You need not do a damn thing . . . just laugh."

THAT NEEDS TO BE RECKONED WITH

This is how the poems sometimes go: One kiss
leads to another.

Maybe I should translate that . . . a few words
of a line appear, and before that line is finished

they have already given birth. That was quick!
What happened to any gestation period?

Yes, sometimes before one poem stops roughing
me up, I discover

there is a whole litter hiding within one phrase
that needs to be reckoned with.

NOT KNOWING EXACTLY WHAT IS GOING ON

You are newly hatched, so when someone
comes by to feed you with some friendship or
even something well cooked,

your beak on occasion sticks them in the neck,
not knowing exactly what is going on.

Even when the Beloved lands on your limb
with a fresh worm of guidance or wisdom,

your clumsiness can persist, and He too gets
poked.

That is why I thought I might keep a safe
distance from you, maybe that *of a few hundred
years*

until you settle down, and get things properly
worked out.

JUST THE WAY I WOULD

The dreams we share of freedom.
The dreams we share of love.

There is such a unison in our every
movement, in our every desire;

we are so alike that I cannot tell the
difference anymore between us.

I could walk into any house and feel
at home,

because you have arranged everything
just the way I would.

JUST BEFORE DAWN

The best time to look for treasure starts
late at night.

The sediment then settles in our sphere,
freed from all the day's hard wants.

One can get a clearer shot at God moving
in the sky forest, just before dawn.

And is there ever a minute, my dear,
when you are not hunting Love?

THE TABLE WHERE YOU ATE

For your sake we are here, not for our own.
Why should I ever complain about working
in the shop where you did?

And the table, earth, where you ate—isn't
that good enough for me?

Your legs stretched out across every particle
of space I might ever encounter; the wise
could build monuments here because of
this.

If my senses were less dull the scent of your
breath would enter me,

for you exhaled something of your soul into
this world, and what you do does last.

For your sake, Beloved, we are here, not for
our own, no matter what directions our
thoughts and actions may turn.

When dawn pulls the veil from my eye, the
scent of your breath will enter me forever,
and lift every sail.

I MIGHT HAVE SEEN AN ABDUCTION

I think this is just what we need to test our
relationship, to see how loyal you really are
to me. So let's talk . . . *flying saucers,*

and maybe I will even hint at an abduction I
might have witnessed, just three nights ago.

They might have gotten you. Are any classic
symptoms showing, like

daydreaming at the wheel and playing with
yourself as you fantasize about supernatural
things?

I hope you are not looking for a cheap way
to fame by saying you made love with an alien.

I did catch one once, in a butterfly net, a UFO,
but thought it best to turn it loose before some

undercover police showed up and thought I
was the ring leader of some . . . exotic coup
d'état.

TWO POEMS FOR THE PRICE OF ONE

Every place where His mouth touched my
body a poem came out.

And there is not one speck of me He did
not kiss.

The above reminds me of some lines I found
that rolled off a mountain and I put in a
sweet ditty called this:

CHERISHED

If you were near darling, I could kiss you
in a way you would feel was perfect,

so perfect it would then protect you from
other kisses . . . that really did not mean it.

I am hoping science evolves soon, soon
enough to where anyone who wants can
carry a simple kind of Geiger counter

that will go off—when any asshole gets
near who might cause trouble.

Because, as I said, I want *to protect you.*
For you are my sweetheart, my pigeon,
my tomato, my dumpling . . . and *all kinds
of things.*

FILL IN THE BLANK

That camel your soul rented from a barn,
you might as well get on good terms with it,
seeing you are out in the wilderness, traveling.

Sometimes I become my own pulse . . . enter
that world inside. There I have stayed a night
marveling at the firmament. Yes, inside any
living thing are stars.

All that the eye sees is just practice for
perfecting . . . the inner vision.

I can't speak anymore of poverty of heart or
purse. For wherever I now stand a gold mine
appears.

How did things change for me, so much for
the better? I held God to His word when He
said, *Seek and you will . . .*

You say that last word for me. You must
know that famous phrase. Believe it, dear,
for it is so very true.

AUGUST 31

WHEN A DOG RUNS UP

Start seeing everything as God, but keep
it a secret.

Become like the man and woman who are
awestruck and nourished

listening to a golden nightingale sing
in a beautiful foreign language while God,
invisible to most, nests upon its tongue.

Hafiz, who can you tell in this world that
when a dog runs up to you wagging its
ecstatic tail, you lean over and whisper in
its ear,

"Beloved, I am so glad you are happy to
see me! Beloved, I am so glad, so very glad
you have come!"

SEPTEMBER

MORE INHERITANCE

Love creates a synchronicity with what love
loves.

Why wouldn't it do that, knowing harmony's
vital role.

The calm heart's reach is vast and lasting.
Bring yourself, again, into the presence of

someone who knows God, for more inheritance
is there for you.

Hold hands with the Buddha, if a living saint's
warmth has been forgotten.

Like a special day when you can naturally feel
uplifted by something in the air, should be a

truth ... we always carry.

A WOMAN HE HELD

Something beautiful, that old green boat
moving slowly in the water.

Something exquisite, that man rowing while
a woman he has held intimately hundreds
of times sits near and rests.

Rests from the wars in the days. Rests from
the wars in the hours. But now, more than
to just relax; she smiles, deeply brightens
and comes alive

as the wing of a duck, landing on the other
side of the pond, *gently touches her cheek.* Yes.

It all seems perfectly natural, realizing that all
dimensions will someday admit . . . we are
your subjects, mere peasants within your vast
kingdom.

All of God, which is everything, is really so
close, and caresses us now and then if your
senses are alert.

The falcon's wing, on my better days, crafts
these images as I watch.

IF A MOUTH THUNDERS

The way my hands can get along with each
other, I now get along with one and all.

Standing in a fierce lightning storm, I look
around and see I am the highest object on
a hill.

Though having become one with the sky,
why would I ever strike myself? What do
I fear from anything?

If any mouth thunders, that sound becomes
sweet.

All rain and hail is very welcomed upon me,
coming from the One Heart as it does.

THE SOLE HEIR TO THE KING

Perhaps for one minute out of the day it
may be of value to torture yourself with
thoughts like,

"I should be doing a hell of a lot more
with my life than I am . . . 'cause I'm so
damn talented."

But remember for just one minute out of
the day.

With all the rest of your time it would be
best to try looking upon yourself more as
God does.

For God knows your true royal nature.
God is never confused and can only *see*
Himself in you.

My dear, Venus just leaned down and
asked me to tell you a secret, to confess

she is just a mirror that has been stealing
your light and music for centuries.

She knows, as does Hafiz, you are the sole
heir to the King.

BEING PLUGGED IN HELPS

It is like finding another position to make
love, coming up with a new poem.

I am surprised at how many ways there
really are.

I guess being plugged into the Infinite helps.

BEHOLD YOUR SELF

Like a great film or play everyone should see,
BEHOLD THYSELF.

Hints of your beauty the mountains have.
The enchanting complexions of the coral reefs
are pale to a golden candle in our heart.

What moves in any ocean moves through us.
A thousand kinds of music play every hour
that you orchestrate.

Let the next ticket you buy help seat you in
front of . . . *your soul.*

YOU MUST HAVE BEEN DRUGGED

If you were my student I would make you
remember this, before I would again let
you near.

I might even have you recite it for a while
whenever we met just to make sure it was
finding a lasting nook in your brain:

Need brings us together; that makes need sacred.
If a person did not have some kind of thirst,
would she ever approach you on her own?

Would his eye ever ask your eye for comfort?
Would his hand ever want to hold yours?

The oasis does not sleep; it is always open; its
very being invites one close; anything you want
from its body, it will say . . . why not?

Though surely amongst us there should be limits
for a while, so that the well can continue to give.

Nevertheless, become an oasis for all things. For
the finite is a tree growing into the infinite.

Golly, on second thought I hope all that is in
italic up yonder, you soon forget!

Hafiz, I don't think you really wrote all this!
You must have been drugged!!!

BUILD A HOUSE FOR MEN AND BIRDS

Build a house for men and birds. Sit with
them and play music.

For a day, for just one day, talk about that
which disturbs no one

and bring some peace, my friend, into your
beautiful eyes.

WHY HEAVEN GETS HIGH MARKS

That simple happiness that comes
from sometimes seeing someone you
want to see—

what is the source of that feeling?
Oh, you know. I talk about it so much.

Why heaven gets such high marks is
because whenever you bump into

anyone there, you always become
delighted.

THERE IS A FACE HERE

Who would want to leave your side, God,
and cause mischief, when you act like that?

Don't you know you could bring an end to
all the pillaging, and so much suffering,

if you just walked through the streets
looking at everyone, as you often now do
toward me?

There is an enchanting face here, between
these words, if you can slow down enough

you will see me, beholding you, beholding
you, in such an extraordinary way.

THOUSANDS ENTER YOUR COURT

Most live in a constant state of comparison.
Thousands enter your court each day, where
you judge.

How many things though get your personal
attention to the extent you might speak to them
or place your hand against their body?

Names and forms are drowning before me.
Sugar and salt blocks were all things, dissolving
now in the Ocean of Light.

Someone calls out for help in the dark, wanting
to remain the limited, wanting to keep the

nightmare intact . . . what should I do, when a
door is now open to return to your self?

INTERESTING THE CLASSROOM

Interesting the classroom where God says,

"Forget all that you think you know about Me."

That way some *real knowledge* might dawn.

HELPING THE DAWN APPEAR

Strange the way my shadow began to fall. I
was standing in a field helping the dawn

appear, and when its body, the sun, was fully
lifted into the sky

I was amazed to see my shadow in *front of
me* as I faced that luminous candle we all know.

I turned around in amazement, wondering
what could possibly be there;

it was the soul, our soul helping God to find
new horizons.

Strange to some, but not to love *evolved*, no
longer any shadow . . . I now cast.

THAT DOES NOT KNOW SADNESS

You entered form to give a holy message.
An envoy from the inconceivable is each
of us.

When you have completed that courageous
task you will be able to return to a world
that does not know sadness.

What is it that you need to say to us, or do?
So difficult your divine errand, it may take

lifetimes to accomplish . . . always loving.
But also, in no way ever being a prude.

KICK BACK AND SAY AHHH

The mind just wants to stop giving a shit
about so many things.

It wants to kick back and say *Ahhh* more.

Not the kind of halfhearted ahhh one might
muster upon request if a doctor just stuck
a forklift down your throat.

There is a lot to a real *Ahhh*. I know you
know that, and thus

you have your *scouts* out looking for "them,"
basically 24-7. Yup, even in your dreams.

"*Them*," of course refers to *Ahhhhhhhhhs*.

IN CASE SOMEONE IS SPYING

I better sound smart once in a while, in case
someone is spying.

What if the truth got out that I really prefer
silliness and silence to offering fancy clues to
the universe?

Maybe I could accomplish both at the same
time the way that Hoopoe over there appears

to be doing . . . as it scratches the ground
looking for a bug in a way that might amuse
the casual onlooker,

but at the same time is really sending out
some covert Morse code

that could have catastrophic results, if I don't
act soon to counterbalance things.

Maybe the moon is really a top secret agent,
up to no good? And has fooled us all . . . for
thousands of years.

WOLF WHISTLE

I think if God stopped controlling Himself
and just gave us all a big *wolf whistle*

That

would

about

cover

it.

MORE LEVERAGE ON STUFF

This is the *wolf whistle refrain,* for such pizzazz and cleverness as that last ditty possessed deserves an encore.

Besides this being a very practical truth, we have a significant *furthermore,* which is: Anyone who seriously contemplates this, meditates upon it for at least nine minutes . . .

could discover they got more leverage on stuff they want to have leverage over.

Sounds useful, the above. So here goes again, that deep preliminary thought:

If God just stopped controlling Himself and gave us all a big *WW*—that would about cover it, *maybe forever and ever and ever.*

THINGS AREN'T SO BAD

Whatever might help you say, *Things aren't so bad* . . . keep as a side-kick.

Maybe even *propose* to anything so useful, if you won't get arrested.

MASTERY IN SERVITUDE

There is really no place for *I can't* in love.
A thought like that goes against the grain
of light's astounding ability.

I saw *caring's* beauty in action; there was
a splendor there I needed to imbibe.

But such a force, *mastery in service*, it tears
you from your moorings,

it will bring you into an arena where a
gladiator you will need to become, but one
that may never get cheered.

Some heroic deed you will do in silence,
for that is greatness's preference—no fame.

If the world comes to know you, be a good
host to the attention you get.

Use all as a tool, dear, to build a shelter for
your mind, and others in need.

THE SIMPLE CHAT

A burning coal against the flesh—who
has not felt this, from news that reached you,

or the shock to your nerves from bearing
eyewitness to horrific events?

The avalanches come, we should help dig
each other out.

The simple chat will return. May it last long,
and be realized as precious.

THE SIZE OF THE LOVE-BRUISE

The gauge of a good poem is . . . *the size
of the love-bruise it leaves on your neck.*

Or the size of the love-bruise it tattoos on
your brain.

Or the size of the love-lump it can weave
into your soul.

Or, indeed, it could be all of the above,
why not?

THE SANDALWOOD TREE

The sandalwood tree shares its lovely scent with
any who come near. God is like that.

Does the tree ever think to itself, *I am not going
to offer my fragrance to that man over there because
of what he did last night,*

*or to that woman who neglected her child, or because
of what we, we might have ever done?*

It is not the way of God to hoard. He is simply
just there, emanating freely what He is, if we wish
to grab a handful, or fill the basket in the eye.

Don't hold back, have no reservations, take full
advantage of His attributes, exploit His nature
and that tender part of His soul.

SEPTEMBER 24

SO ROMANTICALLY

I thought I was on the right track when I
was admiring an odd shaped squash cooking
in a pot and I called it *Angel*.

At least that meant something to me. It
seemed like progress . . .

spontaneously talking in a sweet and
sincere manner to something

that I had not ever spoken to *so romantically,
before.*

THE POEM THAT WAS HERE GOT THE CANE

The poem that was here . . . got the *cane*, it rambled too much, and really said so little that was unique; I think it would have bored you. And why do that?

In its place I will tell you of an experience I just had a minute ago. My right eye felt blurred, and its vision became impaired in an odd, curious way, and I thought *O maybe I am dying. Wonderful.*

I brought myself before a mirror and looked in to see if I might someway help the situation, but instead *saw another me.* How to describe that? Well, I will try.

I was a primal, luminous being in perfect harmony with anything I could conceive. And anything I could conceive I could control, as I was its very creator, its very source. Nothing could ever be in opposition to the truth of myself. All was like at a table God set Himself, with a profound care for His court, that produced an effulgent synergy. I felt like a deity, helping to host a royal event: Existence.

Anything to do with any name or any conventional life was of gigantic insignificance—a colossal fantasy, a child's imaginary, innocent game that could somehow have the strength to veil one from the *Sun* we are.

Though a Sun, now for me, that I can still see and touch whenever I want. It has really been this way for years for me, and the experience can so easily deepen, change, as it never wants to bore. It can't.

MY FAREWELL

Some new texture of consciousness has risen
where I camped.

A fire that I sat around and thought of you,
you turned into a place of pilgrimage that God
visits.

Not bowing to anyone but *yourself*, is where
this world is rightfully heading.

The Beloved is making me the center of His
own being. How can one accept such an office?

Take your greatest moment of pleasure and
multiply that by a millionfold, then you might
barely conceive of what I am talking about.

Has your life been so conservative and restrained
that you never collapsed onto the floor from
ecstasy?

Who can remain standing in this divine process
of turning into God? All forms collapse into a
golden dust.

Nothing of me may survive to speak. These
poems are my farewell. A silence between us

would be my preference, but then my awkward
kiss, my words, might not be known.

CUPPING MY HANDS LIKE A MOUNTAIN VALLEY

Like the way the valleys of the earth cup their
hands for light and drink;

like the way the desert opens up its sweet mouth
and laughs when

someone melts pearls in the sky, and rain, rain
returns like a divine lover with

a hundred wonderful gifts; O the words of the
true teacher now bring to my mind and soul such
a sacred nourishment and life.

Like the way the valleys of the earth cup their
hands for light and drink;

like the way the desert opens up its sweet mouth
and laughs when someone melts pearls in the sky
and rain, rain, rain returns like a divine lover;

hey, I think there is a song here? Go for it!

THEY THOUGHT I WAS
A MARRIAGE COUNSELOR

They thought I was a marriage counselor,
two goats who lived close by.

I had noticed how at times they would
squabble and buck heads, but what couple
doesn't?

When they did one day come to me for
advice I just openly confessed—*It had been*

*quite a while since I had walked around on all
fours and eaten mostly leaves and grass, and
flowers, and paper sometimes.*

That is, I wasn't sure how well I could fully
connect and understand. Still, they wanted
my help, so we started to see each other
once a week.

They are doing better now. And by the way,
I have an opening next Friday, and charge

hardly a thing. You could barter. Maybe bring
an old newspaper, I could hold and turn into
a blaze.

THE BUDDHA STOOD BY AND WATCHED

It is just love and I now, doing whatever
happens.

If someone were to spill some soup upon
me, I would understand, knowing it wanted
to get close the best it could.

All comes your way for a reason. Everything
is working the room and making valuable
connections.

It snowed once, more than it had in years,
above a village in Tibet, and come spring the
temperature climbed way higher than normal.

A tidal wave of slush roared down the mountain
and wiped out many families. The Buddha
stood by and watched, then walked slowly off.

What the average person did not see was
that all those souls dove headfirst into him.
He mixed them in his being. They ran through
his veins shouting with joy.

What could you know of anything if you have
a list of complaints against old friends?

ALLAH KNOWS HIS PLACE

Every day they fall, the leaves, *a body dies*
and sings in a voice few hear.

And every hour life again moves new, a unique
composite of everything, an infant.

All there is placed you in our care. Each of
us should be paraded through the streets,
honored like a visiting prince.

The air, clearer today than I can remember.
There was something about the wind

that was different. It seemed excited about
some grand event it knew for certain,
beforehand, would happen.

I walked into a shop. Feeling overwhelmed
from all the enchantment outside,

I said to the man behind the counter, "God is
great and everywhere today."

And the old merchant responded, "I am
thankful Allah knows His place, His throne,

which is every atom, we too, are made to
sit upon and reign."

OCTOBER

IT HAPPENS ALL THE TIME IN HEAVEN

It happens all the time in heaven, and someday
it will begin to happen again on earth—

that men and women who are married, and
men and men who are lovers,

and women and women who give each other
light,

often will get down on their knees, and while
so tenderly holding their lover's hand, with

tear-filled eyes, will sincerely say, "My dear,
how can I be more loving to you; my darling,

how can I be more kind?"

PERFECT EQUANIMITY

Look how a mirror will reflect with perfect
equanimity all actions before it.

There is no act in this world that will ever
cause the mirror to look away.

There is no act in this world that will ever
make the mirror say "no."

The mirror, like perfect love, will just keep
giving of itself to all before it.

How did the mirror ever get like that, so
polite, so grand, so compassionate?

It watched God.

Yes, the mirror remembers the Beloved
looking into itself, into its being, as the

Beloved shaped existence's heart and the
mirror's soul.

Continued on October 3rd

PERFECT EQUANIMITY (2)

My eye has the nature of God. Hafiz looks
upon all with perfect equanimity, as do my
words, dear.

My poems will never tell you "no," because
the mirror is not like that.

And if God ever hits you with a *don't*—He
has His fingers crossed.

He is just fibbing for your own good.

DROOLING IS A DISADVANTAGE

I know how most minds approach me for the
first time, with caution. And that is wise.
I prefer that behavior over someone drooling
at me like a groupie.

Drooling is a disadvantage in public if one
has healthy and reasonable ambitions in the
world, as I like some of those close to me to
harbor.

Accomplish something with your life; use all
your wits and talents.

Every horse should be able to run full speed,
and know all the beauty and wonder of its
strength.

Win lots of trophies if you can before turning
yourself out to pasture. And if anyone ever
looks at them; O go ahead and tell the truth:
God spurred me, big time. I still have lots of
bruises as proof.

MOUNT SINAI

Mount Sinai sought my counsel last night,
knowing I had become its elder.

They may look like they never have problems,
the planets, but they at times do, like us, and
then look for a friend to talk with.

All things are living, even stones. It has to be
that way; energy pulsates from their bodies,
since all are part of the Omnipresent Living Being.

Everything is holding out their hands, offering
something,

how much easier the world would be to live in if
we were as kind and accepted all. But discernment
should not be abandoned.

The chorus from the peaks will sing in praise
when the Messiah comes again. And He will.

And Mount Sinai will seek your counsel some
night, when you no longer need to sleep.

A MIME

A mime stands upon a gallows for a crime he
did not do. When given a last chance to speak
he remains true to his art.

A crowd of hundreds has gathered to see his
last performance, knowing he will not talk.

The mime takes from the sky the circle of bright
spheres, lays them on a table, expressing deep
love for the companionship and guidance they
have given him for so many years.

He brings the seas before our eyes. Somehow
an emerald fin appears, splashes. Look, there
is turquoise rain.

He removes his heart from his body and seems
to arouse all life on this splendid earth with
such a sacred tenderness;

there, for an extraordinary moment, it looked
like someone was giving birth to the Christ
again.

He mounts his soul upon the body of Freedom.
The great breeze comes by. The sun and moon
join hands; they bow so gracefully

that for a moment, for a moment everyone
knows that God is real. So the tongue fell out
of the mouth of the world for days.

THE CANDLE BURNS DOWN

We melt a little each day. The candle
burns down.

And it may wonder at times, it may
wonder:

What will become of me? What will
happen to my precious flame?

*O, so much brighter, my dear, you will
become, so much brighter.*

BRINGING YOU UP TO DATE

A student of mine who had lost his father at an
early age, and had no uncles or older brothers,
was getting married soon.

And he had never been with a woman before,
so he came to me for advice. He shyly, though
directly, addressed the matter, saying,

"Hafiz, just tell me all I need to know."

I went into some detail about the situation and
even diagrammed a few key points on paper,
knowing I was something of an expert, and feeling
that my wife would wholeheartedly agree.

Tell me all I need to know, I think I heard your heart
say, dear world, about various concerns, and your
pending wedding night with God.

So I have been trying to bring you up to date . . .
the best I can.

I AM REALLY JUST A TAMBOURINE

Good poetry makes the universe admit
a secret: I am really just a tambourine,

grab hold, play me against your warm
thigh.

LIKE THE GANGES

The Sun needs a sacred tablet where it can write its
resplendent verse, and Hafiz has become a blessed
stone.

When the Friend begins to sway from being so full
of wine, music flows like the Ganges from His mouth.

God then needs fertile banks and walls in this world
to govern all that raging light.

I build canals into the cities and into the plains. I
run beside small villages and sing.

I nourish and cool the roots of stars and mankind.
Women wash their clothes in me,

thirsty cattle and skinny dogs come accompanied by
spellbound children, but soon we all begin to splash
and kiss.

Birds fly to my shores, then get excited and spread
the news:

The verse of Hafiz is a wonderful bath; the glance of
Hafiz is a beatific ocean bath

where all can clean their bodies in the sounds of
my lyre and mirth, in the tenderness of my drum's
alluring beat.

Continued on October 11th

LIKE THE GANGES (2)

His music has filled my pores. I am inebriated with
the unbearable Truth.

Tonight I am a staggering, awesome planet, for all
day long I construct alliances

using my divine gravity upon all sinew, minds, and
souls.

I ecstatically speak with words, and also with purest
language—silence—

saying in a thousand different ways: "Dear
countrymen,

all nearby cousins, comets and galaxies, every
amoeba, creature and plant—

bring your cup, bring your cup, and I will pour you
God."

O when the Friend begins to sway from being so
full of love, divine music flows from my mouth.

WHY NOT BE POLITE?

Everyone is really God speaking.
Why not be polite and listen to
the *Old Guy*?

WHAT HARVEST IS EVER GATHERED WITHOUT YOUR HAND?

Who can turn from green to gold without your love?

What harvest is ever gathered without your hand there, Beloved, helping?

God will enter the rhythm of our prayers and remembrance, but first there must be a natural repetition as we go about our holy labor, which is all work on earth.

Graceful motion sings beyond what most pens can offer—at this beautiful feast that moves us always closer to the goal.

I am the mountains' representative. I can speak for them on anyone's behalf. And extend all a vital link you want with their majesty, that you can then adorn yourself with.

A king could change your life in many ways, but not half as much as an *Emperor* like me.

An army is a small toy in God's hand, a breath could come from Him or myself . . . and it would run or fall.

Wise of you to spend time with Hafiz; something is bound to rub off. Or a flea that lives on me might bite you, *and all I have—you catch.*

I THINK THEY HAD A POINT

I overheard some days talking—yes, *days*.
I was at first alarmed, as you might have been,
by what they said.

But then I came to believe they had a point,
which was:

That if they shortened the year by a few
months people would have less time to worry.

Well, as I already wrote . . . *I think they had a
point?* What is your opinion?

SOME ANGELS GRUMBLE

Every time someone on the path does
not keep their word

some angels grumble and have to
remove a few of the bets they had placed

upon that person's heart—to win!

HE YAWNED THIRTY-THREE AND
ONE-HALF TIMES

I sat with him for an hour, a man who kept
insisting I come to his house.

I brought one of my students with me, someone
who I know gets easily bored if the conversation
or thought content . . . ebbs.

This man had in mind to try and impress me
with a thesis he wrote.

I listened as if I never heard anything as great
in my whole life,

which was then confusing to our host, as my
student yawned 33 and 1/2 times and then fell
asleep, expelled foul gas and snored loudly.

All is a kind of learning curve, and perhaps
that man and his pen are still assessing that
night's events.

QUID PRO QUO

I started to feel a couple of years ago that
something just wasn't right, but I couldn't
exactly put my finger on it.

So some silent but tough negotiating ensued
between God and my soul that went on for
a long time. Who could have foretold what
then happened one day?

One afternoon when I was rising in prayer,
having just bowed toward the sacred Kaaba,

God too was rising, with His head just having
touched the ground, facing me.

I could have sworn He said, *Quid pro quo.*

But don't quote me on that. For what would
the mullahs think?

A POETRY WORKSHOP

If I ever gave a poetry workshop here are some key factors I would elaborate upon, hoping to give you your money's worth.

*** Watch out for the word *flower*. It can be lethal.

*** Be equally on your guard for the word *rainbow* and its—for the most part—assault on serious literature.

*** And the words *butterfly* or *star*, I love them, but I think they are best left off the page unless you are desperate, and/or have not yet reached puberty.

That about rounds out the general holy trinity of don'ts in poems, from my perspective.

And if you ever succumb to using the word flower, rainbow, or the *b* or *s* word more than twice in one book, unless it is very cleverly done—well,

well, you should really invite someone to shoot you.

A CHANCE TO PAINT EACH OTHER GOLD

What would make a lover value you over
other lovers they have known?

And tell me about your favorite place to
eat, or the finest meal you ever had.

There is something in *caring touch* that
your memory has recorded . . . and holds
dear, because it nourishes as few things
can.

A sincere wanting and need to artfully
give is inherent in love. And love will
get its way; for patience it knows, and
what a strength that is.

We subtract or add to our beauty with
each movement and sound. Look, we have
a chance to help paint each other gold.

The closest thing to amorous play with
God in form should be the goal of any
intimacy between us.

Us, those who seek that sacred friendship,
and can gaze at each other in appreciation,
in places we allow few to ever see.

AN ARTIST'S BLESSING

Why would a rich man sweep the streets from
morning till night,

and with a broom that causes his back to bend
over to the point of now aching all the time?

There are people like that around, who could
live in a garden paradise and never know of the
common man's suffering,

but instead stay among us, rolling up their sleeves,
drawing from the well until their hands are
blistered and calloused.

They might pass out for a few hours, then get up
early and pick up their pens, chisels, or brushes
again.

Find someone like that, offer help. Next to a
saint, a true artist's blessing can do the most for
this world and you.

THE EARTH'S SILHOUETTES

What plant can grow if you keep lifting it
from the soil?

Let your roots expand unchecked into a vista,
a forest, a river, a song, or some verse you can
hold tenderly.

You need to become quiet for this, as roots
work in silence beneath the earth's silhouettes.

Let all your senses extract from me what
they can. So mineral-rich I am,

having drawn all a soul ever could from what
is above, below and to the side, and within us,
within us my love.

A PIE WHERE YOU LIVE

God brought me to an emerald field and said,
"Harvest me."

As I began to load my wagon with the divine,
from what the sickle moon and I cut,

seeing its extraordinary worth, He spoke again,
saying,

"But don't charge too much for what I gave to
you in exchange for a beautiful prayer."

Not on its own will the meadow seek payment
to be near its soft body;

someone, though, may stand there in a booth
by a gate and make you pay to get close.

It is not like that with me. These words I have
written, that He planted—grind them into a
good bread you can carry as you travel.

Better yet, let them become the delicious amber
crust to a wonderful pie you have, and invite
many others over to eat.

JEALOUS HEARING SOMEONE LAUGH

Have you ever felt jealous hearing someone
laugh? And then began to think to yourself,

"Why am I so caught in the world's snare?
Why don't I know right now the freedom

in other voices when their spirit like an
arrow takes flight above the hour's concern?"

But the heart's laughter is never there to taunt
another, especially if the *other* is feeling low.

Real laughter is a waving, a beckoning, a
message, a calling to all that says,

Over here, come over here for a minute . . .
where things look so different, and you can
have more fun!

IS NOT THE TREASURE?

When love is there, is not the treasure?
When it is not, who could blame a face
that looks sad?

A LOT TO DIGEST

There is a place between knowing you are priceless

and at the same time recognizing you are what is
stepped over in a street

after a horse just left what they do in those
pretty brown clumps, of useful organic matter.

Somewhere between those poles, live if you can.
For anywhere else really won't suit you or serve

a special work that comes to those who
have achieved real equilibrium, a synchronistic
balance with all, all you have ever known.

This may sound like a lot to digest: suns are waiting
to emanate from your pores,

you will have to factor that in someday, I will help
you.

There is a place between knowing you are priceless
and . . .

EVERYONE SHOULD BE HONORED LIKE THIS

When people come to my house for the first time,
if they do not lean toward being too proud,

I will kneel before them and ask for their hand,
and place the back of it against my forehead.

Everyone should be honored like this. What else
can make you grow to your full height?

I am one of God's pillars in this world, and a
proxy too, always carrying out His wish.

And what of those for whom it would be best if
they not see me . . . *humbly* before them—on my
knees, until they are ready?

Well, at night in my prayers, I place my head
upon their feet. I plant, and help awaken, a
sacred realm in all who have entered my mind.

SOMETHING MUST HAVE SPOOKED HIM

He was gallivanting about and seemed to be
having a grand time,

when something must have spooked Him, and
He jumped back into a hole inside of me.

I have been pining ever since, at the rim of many
universes,

not really knowing what to do, wanting to see
God and me so happy like that again, chasing
each other around.

HOW MANY TIMES HAVE YOU FELT
LIKE A CORPSE?

How many times have you felt like a corpse and then came back and told a good joke, that made us all laugh?

And did you ever swear off dancing and then there you were one day, *scooting* about again?

And how many times has your soul felt empty and then maybe . . . a temple for all near you became?

And what of your rare moments when some kind of effulgent wedlock was there, with all in your ken?

Bring those, anything you have cherished, to the forefront of your mind's view, where they belong as a testament to your destiny.

Some pendulum, which you bought a ticket on, rocks this way and that. You can get off. Become more centered.

APPEAR AN EASY MARK AT FIRST

The less friction you make as you move
through this world, the more power you will
gather and can store. Fire will take an interest
in you and think you are an heir to light.

Lightning will start to ride in your purse.
When could you then feel cold? What divine
food could you not prepare, or supply for any?

It is better like this sometimes: Most everyone
starts thinking you are an easy mark, while in
truth, you are just biding your time

waiting for the optimum moment to strike a
lethal blow and make a real difference. But for
that you need forbearance. What lasting
good has ever been rushed?

When you finally speak up or act with passion
you will help tear down some walls of tyranny.

OCTOBER 30

LYING BESIDE MY WIFE

Once when I was awake and lying beside
my wife, she whispered in her sleep, *"Hafiz,
I love you."*

I don't think I would trade having heard her
soul speak that way, even for all of heaven
saying the same thing.

But is there a difference? I think *loving* is
always God, showing us *It* is here, as much
as the formless can reach into our world.

AN OLD MUSICIAN

How do those who know of God meet
and part? Like the way an old musician
will greet his beloved instrument

and will take special care, the way a great
artist always does, to enhance the final
note of each performance.

NOVEMBER

NOVEMBER

YOU'RE IT

God, disguised as a myriad things and
playing a game of tag,

has kissed you and said, "You're it—
I mean you're Really IT!"

Now it does not matter what you believe
or feel,

for something wonderful, major-league
wonderful, is someday going to

happen.

CAST ALL YOUR VOTES FOR DANCING

I know the voice of depression still calls to
you.

I know those habits that can ruin your life
still send their invitations.

But you are with the Friend now and look
so much stronger.

You can stay that way and even bloom!
Keep squeezing drops of the Sun

from your prayers and work and music and
from your companions' beautiful laughter.

Keep squeezing drops of the Sun from the
sacred hands and glance of your Beloved

and, my dear, from the most insignificant
movements of your own holy body.

Learn to recognize the counterfeit coins
that may buy you just a moment of pleasure

but then drag you for days like a broken
man behind a farting camel.

Continued on November 3rd

CAST ALL YOUR VOTES FOR DANCING (2)

You are with the Friend now. Learn what
actions of yours delight Him,

what actions of yours bring freedom and
love.

Whenever you say God's name, dear
pilgrim, my ears wish my head was missing

so they could finally kiss each other and
applaud all your nourishing wisdom!

O keep squeezing drops of the Sun from
your prayers and work and music

and from your companions' beautiful
laughter, and from the most insignificant

movements of your own holy body. Now,
sweet one, be wise.

Cast all your votes for dancing!

BECAUSE OF OUR WISDOM

In many parts of the world water is scarce and precious.

People sometimes have to walk a great distance, then carry heavy jugs upon their heads.

Because of our wisdom, we will travel far for love. All movement is a sign of thirst.

Most speaking really says, "I am hungry to know you."

Every desire of your body is holy; every desire of your body is holy.

Dear one, why wait until you are dying to discover that divine truth?

SHE RESPONDED

The birds' favorite songs you do not hear,
for their most flamboyant music takes place

when their wings are stretched above the
trees and they are smoking the opium of

pure freedom. It is healthy for the prisoner
to have faith

that one day he will again move about
wherever he wants;

feel the wondrous grit of life—less structured—
find all wounds, debts stamped, canceled, paid.

I once asked a bird, "How is it that you fly
in this gravity of darkness?"

She responded, "Love lifts me."

MY EYES SO SOFT

Don't surrender your loneliness so quickly.
Let it cut more deep.

Let it ferment and season you as few human
or even divine ingredients can.

Something missing in my heart tonight has
made my eyes so soft, my voice so tender,

my need of God absolutely clear.

WITH THAT MOON LANGUAGE

Admit something: Everyone you see, you
say to them, "Love me."

Of course you do not say this out loud;
otherwise someone would call the cops.

Still, though, think about this, this great
pull in us to connect.

Why not become the one who lives with
a full moon in each eye

that is always saying, with that sweet
moon language,

what every other eye in this world is dying
to hear?

CASTRATING AN EGO

The only problem with not castrating a
gigantic ego is that it

will surely become amorous and father a
hundred screaming ideas and kids

who will then all quickly grow up and
skillfully proceed to run up

every imaginable debt and complication
of which your brain can conceive.

This would concern normal parents and
any seekers of freedom

and the local merchants nearby as well.

They could very easily become forced
to disturb your peace;

all those worries and bills could turn to
wailing ghosts.

The only problem with not lassoing a
runaway ego is

you won't have much desire to play in
this sweet world.

HOW FASCINATING

How fascinating the idea of death can be.
Too bad, though, because *it just isn't true.*

LAUGHTER

What is laughter? What is laughter? It is God
waking up! O it is God waking up!

It is the sun poking its sweet head out from
behind a cloud you've been carrying too long,
veiling your eyes and heart.

It is light breaking ground for a great structure
that is your real body—called Truth.

It is happiness applauding itself and then taking
flight to embrace everyone and everything in this
world.

Laughter is the polestar held in the sky by our
Beloved, who eternally says,

"Yes, dear ones, come this way, come this way
toward Me and Love!

Come with your tender mouths moving and your
beautiful tongues conducting songs

and with your movements—your magic movements
of hands and feet and glands and cells—dancing!

Know that to God's eye, all movement is a wondrous
language, and music—such exquisite, wild music!"

O what is laughter, Hafiz? What is the precious
love and laughter budding in our hearts?

It is the glorious sound of a soul waking up!

BEAUTIFUL HANDS

This is the kind of Friend you are:

Without making me realize my soul's
anguished history,

you slip into my house at night and,
while I am sleeping,

you silently carry off all my suffering
and sordid past in your beautiful
hands.

IT CUTS THE PLOW REINS

What does purity do? It cuts the plow reins.
It keeps you from working and dining in the
mud.

It frees you from living behind a big ox that
bites.

What can purity do, my dear? It can lift your
heart on a rising, bucking Sun that makes the
soul hunger to reach the roof of creation.

It offers what the whole world wants: real
knowledge and power.

It offers what the wise crave: the priceless
treasure of freedom.

Pure divine love is no meek priest or tight
banker;

it will smash all your windows and only then
throw in the holy gifts.

Continued on November 13th

IT CUTS THE PLOW REINS (2)

It will allow you to befriend life and light and
sanity and not even mind waking to another
day.

It reveals the excitement of the present and
the beauty of precision.

It confers vitality and a sublime clarity until
finally

all the heart can do is burst open with great
love and cheer!

O purity, O dear truth and friend within me,
why didn't you tell me sooner you could do
all this—

cut the reins of illusion, so we can all just go
wild, loving God and everyone all day!

SEVERAL TIMES IN THE LAST WEEK

Ever since happiness heard your name, it has
been running through the streets trying to find
you.

And several times in the last week, God Himself
has even come to my door—asking me for your
address!

Once I said, "God, I thought You knew everything.
Why are you asking me where Your lovers live?"

And the Beloved replied, *Indeed, Hafiz, I do know
everything—but it is fun playing dumb once in
a while.*

*And I love intimate chat and the warmth of your
heart's fire.*

Maybe we should make this poem into a song—
I think it has potential!

How does this refrain sound, for I know it is a
truth:

Ever since happiness heard your name, it has
been running through the streets trying to find
you.

And several times in the last week, God Himself
has come to my door—

so sweetly asking for your address, wanting the
beautiful warmth of your heart's fire.

THE SUBJECT TONIGHT IS LOVE

The subject tonight is love, and for tomorrow
night as well.

As a matter of fact, I know of no better topic
for us to discuss until we all die!

THE QUINTESSENCE OF LONELINESS

I am like a heroin addict in my longing for
a sublime state, for that ground of Conscious
Nothing where the Rose ever blooms.

O, the Friend has done me a great favor and
so thoroughly ruined my life; what else would
you expect seeing God would do!

Out of the ashes of this broken frame there
is a noble rising son pining for death, because
since we first met, Beloved,

I have become a foreigner to every world
except that one in which there is only You—
or Me.

Now that the heart has held that which can
never be touched, my subsistence is a blessed
desolation, and from that I cry for more
loneliness.

I am lonely. I am so lonely, dear Beloved, for
the quintessence of loneliness. For what is more
alone than God?

Hafiz, what is more pure and alone, what is as
magnificently sovereign as God?

ELOQUENT PETITIONS AND CLEVER COMPLAINTS

I have seen You heal a hundred deep wounds
with one glance from Your spectacular eyes,

while Your hands beneath the table pour large
bags of salt into the heart-gashes of Your most
loyal servants.

Dear world, I can offer an intelligent explanation
for our spiritual suffering . . . but I hope it really
makes sense to no one here

and come morning you are again at God's door
with ax and pickets, eloquent petitions and
very clever, loud complaints.

Think of suffering as being washed. That is to
say, Hafiz, you are often completely soaked and
dripping.

The only advantage I can see in this, in the Friend's
long-range plan, is that when the Beloved bursts
into ecstatic flames

the whole world will not turn into a bright oil wick
all at once—and then divine ash, and thus ruin

His winter crop; which is most of us. I mean our
big yield is probably somewhere down the road,
in the futures market.

Oh well.

FORGIVENESS IS THE CASH

Forgiveness is the cash you need. All the other
kinds of silver really buy just strange things.

Everything has its music. Everything has the
genes of God inside.

But learn from those courageous addicted lovers
of glands and ganja and gold—

look, they cannot jump high or chuckle long
when they are whirling.

And the moon and the stars become sad when
their tender light is used for night wars.

Forgiveness is part of the treasure you need to
craft your falcon wings

and return to your true realm, our true realm
of divine freedom.

SAINTS BOWING IN THE MOUNTAINS

Do you know how beautiful you are? I think not,
my dear. For as you talk of God,

I see great parades with colorful bands streaming
from your mind and heart,

carrying wonderful and secret messages to every
corner of this world.

I see saints bowing in the mountains, hundreds
of miles away, to the wonder

of sounds that break into light from your most
common words.

Speak to me of your mother, your father, your
cousins, and your friends.

Tell me of animals and birds you know. Awaken
your legion of wings—let them soar wild and free
in the sky

and begin to sing to God. Let's all begin to sing
to God!

Do you know how beautiful you are? I think not,
my dear.

Yet Hafiz could set you upon a stage and worship
you forever!

ALL THE HEMISPHERES

Leave the familiar for a while. Let your senses
and bodies stretch out

like a welcomed season onto meadows and
shores and hills.

Open up to the roof. Make a new watermark
on your excitement and love.

Like a blooming night flower, bestow your vital
fragrance of happiness and giving upon our
intimate assembly.

Change rooms in your mind for a day. All the
hemispheres in existence lie beside an equator
in your soul.

Greet yourself in your thousand other forms as
you mount the hidden tide and travel back home.

All the hemispheres in heaven are sitting around
a campfire chatting, while

stitching themselves together into the *great circle*
inside of you.

JUST LOOKING FOR TROUBLE

I once had a student who would sit alone

in his house at night shivering with anxiety
and fear.

And come morning, he would often look as
though he had been raped by a ghost.

Then one day my compassion crafted him a
knife from my own divine sword.

Since then, I have become very proud of this
student.

For now, come evening, not only has he lost
all his apprehensions;

now he goes out just looking for trouble.

I HAVE COME INTO THIS WORLD TO SEE THIS

I have come into this world to see this:

the sword drop from men's hands even at the height
of their arc of anger

because we have finally realized there is just one
flesh to wound and it is His—the Christ's, our Beloved's.

I have come into this world to see this: all creatures
holding hands as we pass through this miraculous

existence we share on the way to even a greater being
of soul,

a being of just ecstatic light, forever entwined and at
play with Him.

I have come into this world to hear this: every song
the earth has sung since it was conceived in the
Divine's womb

and began spinning from His wish, every song by wing
and fin and hoof, every song by hill and tree and
woman and child;

Continued on November 23rd

I HAVE COME INTO THIS WORLD
TO SEE THIS (2)

every song of stream and rock, every song of tool and
lyre and flute, every song of gold and emerald and fire,

every song the heart should cry with magnificent dignity
to know itself as God;

for all other knowledge will leave us again in want and
aching—only imbibing the glorious Sun will complete
us.

I have come into this world to experience this: women
and men so true to love they would rather die before
speaking an unkind word,

women and men so true their lives are His covenant—
the promise of hope.

I have come into this world to see this:

the sword drop from men's hands even at the height
of their arc of rage

because we have finally realized, we have finally realized,
there is just one flesh we can wound and it is *our own.*

I KNOW THE WAY YOU CAN GET

I know the way you can get when you have not
had a drink of Love;

your face hardens, your sweet muscles cramp.
Children become concerned about a strange

look that appears in your eyes which even
begins to worry your own mirror and nose.

Cats sense your sadness and call an important
conference in a tall tree.

They decide which secret code to chant to help
your mind and soul.

Even angels fear that brand of madness that
arrays itself against the world

and throws sharp stones and spears into the
innocent and into one's self.

O I know the way you can get if you have not
been out drinking Love:

You might rip apart every sentence your friends
and teachers say, looking for hidden clauses.

You might weigh every word on a scale like a
dead fish.

Continued on November 25th

I KNOW THE WAY YOU CAN GET (2)

You might pull out a ruler to measure from every
angle in your darkness

the beautiful dimensions of a heart you once
trusted.

I know the way you can get if you have not had
a drink from Love's hands.

That is why all the Great Ones speak of the vital
need to keep remembering God,

so you will come to know and see Him as being
so giving and wanting, just wanting to help.

That is why Hafiz says, "Bring your cup near me,
for I am a Sweet Old Vagabond with an

infinite leaking barrel of Light and Laughter and
Truth that the Beloved has tied to my back.

Dear one, indeed, please bring your heart near
me. For all I care about is quenching your thirst
for freedom!

All a sane man can ever care about is giving
Love!"

YOU DON'T HAVE TO ACT CRAZY ANYMORE

You don't have to act crazy anymore; we all
know you were good at that.

Now retire, my dear, from all that hard work
you do

of bringing pain to your sweet eyes and heart.

Look in the clear mountain mirror—see the
beautiful ancient warrior

and the divine elements you always carry
inside

that infused this universe with sacred life so
long ago

and that join you eternally with all existence—
with God!

You don't have to act nuts anymore; we all
know . . . *you were good at that, now and then.*

GO FOR A WALK IF IT IS NOT TOO DARK

Go for a walk, if it is not too dark. Get some
fresh air; try to smile.

Say something kind to a safe-looking stranger,
if one happens by.

Always exercise your heart's knowing. You might
as well attempt something real along this path:

Take your spouse or your lover into your arms
the way you did when you first met.

Let tenderness pour from your eyes the way the
Sun gazes warmly on the earth.

Start a game with some children. Extend yourself
to a friend.

Sing a few ribald songs to your pets and plants—
why not let them get drunk and loose?

Let's toast every rung we've climbed on evolution's
ladder.

Whisper, *"I love you! I love you!"* to the whole mad
world.

Let's stop reading about God—we will never
understand Him.

Jump to your feet, wave your fists, threaten and
warn the whole universe

that your heart can no longer live without real
and lasting feelings!

NOW IS THE TIME

Now is the time to know that all you do is
sacred.

Now, why not consider a lasting truce with
yourself and God?

Now is the time to understand that all your
ideas of right and wrong were just

a child's training wheels, to be laid aside when
you could finally live with veracity and courage.

Hafiz is a divine envoy whom the Beloved has
written a holy message upon.

My dear, please tell me, why do you still throw
sticks at your heart and Him?

What is it in that sweet voice inside that incites
you to fear?

Now is the time for the world to know that every
thought and action is sacred.

This is the time for you to deeply compute the
impossibility that there is anything but Grace.

Now is the season to know that everything we
do . . . is sacred.

THERE IS A WONDERFUL GAME

There is a game we should play, and it goes
like this:

We hold hands and look into each other's
eyes and scan each other's face.

Then I say, "Now tell me a difference you
see between us."

And you might respond, "Hafiz, your nose
is ten times bigger than mine!"

Then I would say, "Yes, my dear, almost ten
times!"

But let's keep playing. Let's go deeper, go
deeper.

For if we do, our spirits will embrace and
interweave,

our union will be so glorious that even God
will not be able to tell us apart.

There is a wonderful game we should play
with everyone and it goes, it goes *like this* . . .

EACH SOUL COMPLETES ME

My Beloved said, "My name is not complete
without yours."

And I thought: How could a human's worth
ever be such?

And God, knowing all our thoughts, and all
our thoughts are just innocent steps on the

path, then addressed my heart,

God revealed a sublime truth to the world
when He sang,

"I am made whole by your life. Each soul, each
soul completes Me."

DECEMBER

THIS PLACE WHERE YOU ARE RIGHT NOW

This place where you are right now, God circled
on a map for you.

Wherever your eyes and arms and heart can move
against the earth and sky, the Beloved has bowed
there,

the Beloved has bowed there *knowing* you were
coming.

I could tell you a priceless secret about your real
worth, dear pilgrim,

but any unkindness to yourself, any confusion
about others, will keep one from accepting the
grace,

the love, the sublime freedom Divine Knowledge
always offers to you.

Never mind, Hafiz, about the great requirements
this path demands of the wayfarers,

for your soul is too full of wine tonight to withhold
the wondrous truth from this world. But because
I am so clever and generous,

I have already clearly woven a resplendent lock of
His tresses as a remarkable gift in this verse for you.

This place where you are right now, God circled on
a map. And wherever, dear, you can move against

this earth and sky, the Beloved has bowed there,
knowing, knowing you were coming.

NOTHING CAN SHATTER THIS LOVE

Nothing can shatter this love.
For even if you took another

into your arms, the truth is,
my sweetheart, you would

still

be

kissing

me.

THE SEASON EXISTENCE

I like the way you blush, God,
the season spring,

the season summer, the season
fall, the hour of winter,

and that magnificent season
existence!

Yes, I love the way you blush, my
Lord, when we are sometimes
near.

CHARGING GOD RENT

I might have to start charging God rent
unless He starts doing more around the
house,

other than remaining locked, for the most
part, in a room in me, and playing hard to
get.

Seems He could at least wash a few dishes
and pick up a broom once in a while in view
of . . .

*Look at who is paying all the bills around here.
You're damn right, it's me!*

THE SHAPE OF COLOR

The shape of night, the shape of day, the shape
of color, the shape of us. What holds all this?

Who made this miraculous mold and then too,
cast everything?

Imagine the form that poured all forms, and
then try to conceive the Being

that whittled out the Holy Spirit from a single
thought that took over the Inconceivable.

What can entwine all this in its arms ? What a
container there must be that some, still *hung
up on names*, call . . . God.

An atheist would not last long in front of my
Beloved, as soon as His lips touched theirs,

we could have one more religious fanatic to deal
with.

MAKE A GOOFY FACE

Fear likes a moving target. If a tiger were chasing
you, your only chance of survival might be

to stop, turn around, and look into its eyes; then
stick your thumbs in your ears and wiggle your
fingers. You might as well try anything in a

desperate situation, and that seems perilous
indeed—a wild beast's drooling jaws in your
vicinity.

Yes, as a last option, make a goofy face. This
could be befitting to situations in life in general.

And fear, if it thinks it can't take root in you,
will go somewhere else for easier pickings.

Most roots like something still and undisturbed
to grow in. There are always various aspects of
nature at play that parallel their parent—
metaphysical laws.

Sit down with a name of God on your tongue,
or let your spirit arms reach within and embrace
something sacred there; you might begin to shine.

All that lives in shadows, all names and forms,
will then run from—or bow to—the king of the
jungle . . . your soul, your soul.

AND WHEN SHE BEGAN TO SING

And then she began to sing, and when
she began to sing,

there was no one who really heard her
who was not then glad to be alive.

OF COURSE THINGS LIKE THAT CAN HAPPEN

God once made love to a saint who had a hairy belly. Of course things like that can happen!

And it was a surprise, only to the novice on the path, when the saint's stomach began to swell just like a woman's.

Weeks went by, then months. The saint's cheeks blossomed into beautiful roses. He became like a young bride, pregnant with a holy child. His gratitude was speechless, and his eyes shone like two planets making love.

The town began to stand outside his house at night, for it had come to the attention of the faithful that as the moon passed by on its round, it would sometimes bend over and kiss his roof! Of course things like that can happen.

Life went on, amidst the ten thousand other wonders: Whiskers and weeds and trees and charming babies kept emerging.

People and cattle and bees worked side by side, all sweetly humming.

And come lunch, all dined on the same mysterious divine manna of nourishing Love—disguised in a thousand shapes, colors and forms.

Galaxies gave away their ingenious ideas and told us of their private body functions. So man too, eats, burps and excretes more worlds.

How is it that invisible thoughts can lift heavy matter and build cities and armies and altars?

All contain a hidden strategy to be transformed again into the holy wonderment!

Continued on December 9th

OF COURSE THINGS LIKE THAT CAN HAPPEN (2)

The sun rolls through the sky meadow every day and a billion cells run to the top of a leaf to scream and applaud and smash things in their joy.

Of course things like that can happen.

Rivers stay up all night and chant; luminous fish jump out of the water spitting emeralds at all talk of heaven being anywhere else, but—Right Here!

Clouds pull each other's pants down and point and laugh. Oh my dear, of course things like that can happen. For all is written in the mind to help and instruct the dervish in dance, romance and prayer.

The stars get a little crazy and drunk at night and throw themselves across the sky.

Only an insane compound is not going mad with excitement at this extraordinary performance by God!

And still, light stretches its arms open even more and calls to you because you are creation's lover, to cease any unforgiving and just boogie—O yeah! Look! Angels and flowers are playing hooky in graveyards, laughing and rolling naked on cool stones.

Why go to sleep tonight, exhausted from fear or want when the Old King, Himself, is still so jazzed up—He is doing somersaults and handstands, and offering useful advanced lessons . . . about stuff between the sky & earth's sheets.

Hell yes, O boy, O girl—indeed things like that can happen.

Continued on December 10th

OF COURSE THINGS LIKE THAT CAN HAPPEN (3)

A few days before the delivery of God's baby, the saint had to visit a city close by where few knew of him.

He was walking unnoticed past a mosque, and the shouts of God's admirers happened to fill the air, saying, "Allah, Allah! Where are You? Reveal Thyself, Beautiful, Precious One."

And the child in the womb of the Master could not remain silent, and sang back, in an astounding voice,

"I Am Here! I Am Here—dear life!"

The crowd in the mosque became frantic, and they picked up shoes, clubs and stones. You know what then happened—the story becomes grim. For most cannot bear the truth.

But the moon cannot hold a grudge. It still stops by some nights and leans over this holy earth and gives each object and creature . . . a full, wet kiss.

For the moon knows that God is amorous deep down—He cannot stop making love.

From the Unseen and Immaculate we came for a visit to form. All of heaven, and every world, is but a footstool before our true and lasting throne.

O Hafiz, look at the splendor of God's kindness: The sun, His Self, has been planted in a thousand furrows across every soul's body.

Of course my sweet ones, everything God and I say, can happen.

Continued from December 9th

FIDDLING WITH THE IDIOT & HOPEFUL

Once when I was fussing with my hair in front
of a looking glass, my master walked by and
said,

Hafiz, why are you always fiddling with the idiot?
You should starve him a day or two now and then.
Simply don't look in a mirror.

Once a week I started abstaining from vanity.
No mirror.

Then I went to twice a week, then four times.
Then a little bird started to build a nest in
my beard and let out melodious chants in the
morning.

It was then I realized I was probably onto
something big . . . and began walking around
looking very hopeful.

I WISH I COULD SPEAK LIKE MUSIC

I wish I could speak like music. I wish I could put
the swaying splendor of fields into words so that

you could hold Truth against your body and dance.
I am trying the best I can with this crude brush,

the tongue, to cover you with light. I wish I could
speak like divine music. I want to give you the

sublime rhythms of this earth and the sky's limbs
as they joyously spin and surrender, surrender

against God's luminous breath. Hafiz wants you
to hold me against your precious body and dance,
dance.

OPEN THE DOOR OR DIE

There is an invisible sun we long to see. The closer
you get to the present, the brighter and more
real it will become, even at midnight.

To the poor slaves of this world with their
eyes chained to coins and unforgiving, the
wondrousness of the firmament can cease to lift
your head and impact your manners.

What wing would not become depressed within
a snare, if that wing still has some spirit in it,
and all your instincts to want to taste that
stratosphere above the known?

"Open the door or die. Unlock the cage or die."
My master would to say to me, when I was young.

THE BEST I CAN DO FOR MORAL ADVICE

Anyone you have made love with, it is because
you were really looking for God.

If you have known hundreds of partners, God
may not say this publicly, but I think He is
proud of all your efforts.

Don't let the freedom in this truth get you in
trouble.

There are men out there who get lonely up in the
hills and then *take it out* on their camels, sheep
and goats.

I think about the best I can do today along the
lines of moral advice, in such a universe as we
live, is to say,

try to not hurt any living thing, 'cause your odds
will then, probably, increase for happiness—and
who doesn't want some of that?

WHAT GOOD IS A BOOK OF POEMS?

What good is a book of my poems if you are
reading it while riding

in the back of a wagon that is heading toward
the edge of a cliff?

A greater awareness is what our relationship
is supposed to be about.

I was hoping something I might have said by
now could have made you stop, get your bearings,

and start traveling in a direction that will yield
lots of fruit. Maybe you are? That would be nice.

OUT OF THE MOUTHS OF
A THOUSAND BIRDS

Listen, listen more carefully to what is around you
right now.

In my world there are the bells from the clanks
of the morning milk drums

and a wagon wheel outside my window just hit a
bump,

which turned into an ecstatic chorus of the Beloved's
Name.

And there is the Prayer Call rising up like the sun
out of the mouths of a thousand birds.

There is an astonishing vastness of movement and
life emanating sound and light

from my folded hands, and my even quieter simple
being and heart.

My dear, is it true that your mind is sometimes like
a battering ram

running all through the city and the villages
shouting

so madly inside and out about the hundreds of things
that do not matter?

Continued on December 17th

OUT OF THE MOUTHS OF
A THOUSAND BIRDS (2)

Hafiz, too, for many years beat his head in youth
and thought

himself at a great distance, far from an armistice
with God.

But that is why this scarred old pilgrim has now
become such a sweet rare vintage who weeps and
plays a drum for you.

That is why Hafiz will forever in his verse play his
cymbal and sing to you.

O listen, O listen more carefully to what is around
you right now.

In my world all that remains is the wondrous call
to dance and prayer

rising up like a thousand suns, out of the mouth
of a single bird.

LOW-KEY

Think of all the attention a donkey would get if it started to speak more eloquently and make more sense than everyone else for miles around.

With that in mind I hold back a lot. Because I like to fit in, usually. *Act low-key.*

Am I doing so now, appearing normal? It is getting hard sometimes. For God keeps ooooooooozing through my cracks.

ABOUT BEING MORE SECURE

They touch us, don't they? So many things in different ways. And then those feelings can last for years in varying degrees.

Are not our days and hours our response to what we have felt?

We circle inside what we love, what we fear, what we hope.

The mind is like a falcon, ever ready with its sight on its choice prey—beauty. For nothing satisfies like Her taste.

A holy infant, taken from God's womb, is each creature.

What happened to your royal attendant? Who allowed you to crawl to places that can give you the feeling, at times, of dread?

This poem was longer by some 20 lines, but I let them go back to where they came from, some shop in the ethers.

There's enough here to contemplate, as is. My humming is winding down. My favorite season of love has approached . . . quiet.

Most live before dawn and become overwhelmed with the frightening noises, ideas, in your house and mind.

You know what I mean, about being more secure with *the light on.*

ON THE VERGE OF A BAD DEAL

There is not a waking moment that you are
not trying to savor what you have, or get closer
to what will bring you pleasure.

Being so preoccupied as we are with needing to be
satisfied, it seems we would be better at it by now:

that happiness would be our norm, not a rare event.

No heart can make love to its source and then can
turn its back on the Truth of your destiny . . . which
is someday—you will never again know pain,

moreover *be* the very fountainhead of all dance,
laughter, eloquence.

Hafiz, why do you say all the things that you do?
Well, angels, I sometimes see you standing in the

market place on the verge of a bad deal. I see
someone convincing your wings to build a house

on earth, but your wings are not really meant for
that. Thus how could sorrow then not come?

With your money in hand, about to sign some
contract, if a charming minstrel came by, singing
in a jovial mood,

you might turn in his direction and for another
moment be spared the world's cruel bindings.

There is not a word I have written that does not
hope for your freedom and contain the ingredients
for it.

RICHES EVERYWHERE

Don't envy my talents, or seek them.
For few could bear the suffering it took
to mine the jewels I have brought to town.

There are divine riches everywhere. The
most natural way for most to find them
is by caring for those who are close to
you as if they were our Beloved.

STILL WRAPPED

"But I don't look like a sun,"

a young star still wrapped in swaddling
veils said.

To which I replied,

"But you will, my dear. You will, mashuq.*
So don't worry. Don't fret."

---

* Mashuq: Thought you might as well learn a nice Persian word. It can mean, *beloved and/or sweetheart.* Cause, I bet, you . . . *is,* and or—*are!*

A PRAYER I SOMETIMES SAY

It is the Beloved who is revealed in every
face, sought in every sign,

gazed upon by every eye, worshipped in
every object that is adored, pursued in the
visible and in the unseen.

Not a single one of His creatures, not a
single one, my dears, will

fail to someday find the divine Source
in all of its primordial and glorious nature.

And be forever united with the Infinite,
because *that—God—is really you.*

Muhyiddin Ibn 'Arabi, look what your
words have become—the restoration of
Truth, the regeneration of Life itself.

IBN 'ARABI AND THE CHRIST

I remember the first time I ever heard my master recite the verse of Ibn 'Arabi. It was Christmas day. And my master said this poem, in part, describes the consciousness of Mohammad, Jesus, Buddha and anyone who achieves union with *the Rose*, with God. I knew something of this poem but my master spoke it differently, adding to it as one might to a song they were playfully singing. Later that night he said it again, though very seriously and in a remarkable atmosphere. The room was candlelit. The verse was accompanied by some music he asked me to play. And while Attar spoke these words, he began to weep in ecstasy; it was the only time I ever saw him do that.

> *My heart holds within it all form, that my heart created.*
> *I have made a pasture there for gazelles and children.*
>
> *Within me is a true monastery for monks of every creed.*
> *There, I pledge perfect obedience to Light, and when any*
> *vows are broken or a shadow you enthrone, I am to blame,*
> *who else? All acts enrich us—though be careful in this*
> *realm of thought, of freedom.*
>
> *Where I have allowed the Inconceivable to appear and*
> *pretend it has a name or shape—churches, temples and*
> *mosques are built and obscure the Indivisible. Holy books*
> *were written trying to describe a mere kiss on the cheek*
> *God and I gave this earth.*
>
> *The only real Sufi is one who turns into the root of my soul,*
> *and discovers every religion pays us homage. This is not*
> *blasphemy, all other experience is. But keep this a secret*
> *from a crazed mind with a stone in its hand.*

Continued on December 25th

IBN 'ARABI* AND THE CHRIST (2)

*Whisper softly the word love if you do not have the strength
to let it annihilate you in silence. Burn into the Illumined
Immaculate Nothing where paradise draws itself from a well
you dug.*

*A thousand shields you hold up against Allah and other
human beings, because your surrender to Knowledge is
not ripe. The Sun smiles though upon any who wave a
sword at it, knowing it is safe from harm, as is your essence.*

*Don't let your golden wings suffer, let them taste the Beloved's
lips; there is something in your heart that can lift them into
the Sky's oasis.*

*The galaxies you invented. The firmament is a nest you once
built. When existence hatched you brought us food of divinity.*

*Our heart holds within it all forms, that our hearts created.
We have made a meadow there for gazelles, children, music,
dance and dreams.*

---

* Muhyiddin Ibn 'Arabi (1165–1240) is considered by many to be one of the world's great spiritual teachers. Ibn 'Arabi was born in Murcia, Al-Andalus (Spain). His writings have had an immense impact throughout the Islamic countries and now beyond; it is said his work greatly influenced Dante's. The universal ideas within his poetry, philosophical and theological writings, are believed by scholars to be a vital and timely "bridge between the worlds" like the works of Rumi and Hafiz. To some, Ibn 'Arabi is believed to have achieved the state of perfection or Christ Consciousness. His tomb-shrine, in Damascus, is a place of sacred pilgrimage.

EVERYTHING I HAVE IS ALSO YOURS

There are so many gifts still unopened from your
birthday. There are so many hand-crafted presents
that have been sent to your door by God.

The Beloved does not mind repeating, *"Everything I
have is also yours."*

So forgive Hafiz and the Friend if we break into a
sweet laughter when your heart complains of being
thirsty . . . when ages ago, every cell in your
body capsized forever into His infinite golden sea.

A lover's pain is like holding one's breath too long
in the middle of a vital performance, in the middle
of one of Creation's favorite songs.

Indeed, a lover's pain is this sleeping, this sleeping
when God just rolled over and gave you such a big
good-morning smooch.

There are so many gifts still unopened from your
soul's birthday. There are so many hand-crafted
presents that have been sent into your life by God.

And the Beloved does not mind at all repeating,

"Everything I have is also yours."

DROPPING KEYS

The small man builds cages for everyone
he knows,

while the sage, who has to duck his head
when the moon is low,

keeps dropping keys all night long for the
beautiful, rowdy prisoners.

THE TENDER MOUTH OF THE EARTH

What will the burial of my body be? The
pouring of a sacred cup of wine into the earth's

tender mouth and making my dear sweet lover
laugh one more time.

What is the passing of a body? The glorious
lifting of the spirit into the sacred arms of the

Sky, and making existence smile, one more, *one
more time*.

A RIVER UNDERSTANDS

I used to know my name. Now I don't. I
think a river understands me.

For what does it call itself in that blessed
moment when it starts emptying into the
Infinite Luminous Sea,

and opening every aspect of self wider than
it ever thought possible?

Each drop of itself now running to embrace
and unite with a million new friends.

And you were there, in my union with All,
everyone who will ever see this page.

THE TERRAIN AROUND HERE

Out of a great need we are holding hands and climbing.
Not loving is a letting go.

Listen, the terrain around here is far too steep and
dangerous for that.

BE NOT GRIEVED*

Although you have not received love's true guerdon, one
day your desert will become a garden, so be not grieved.

Do not turn your heart away, nor speak against your
Beloved, but bear your present state, and be not grieved.

Let your tender, wincing body and troubled mind be
stilled; one day desire for union will be fulfilled, so be
not, O dear one, be not grieved.

Behind the curtain a secret, wondrous game is being
played, that you know not, so do not give up, nor be
dismayed, or grieved.

Once you have found the courage to set out for the
Sun's abode, do not let any fears turn you from this
sacred road, or be, or ever be much grieved.

Maya will do her best to thwart your precious labor
on this path, but when you have a captain like Noah
you will reach safe harbor, so be not grieved.

The True Teacher is really the same as God, so don't
plague him with petitions or clever complaints, but
suffer gladly love's paradox, rules, trials and conditions,
and my darling, O my darlings . . . yes, be not grieved.

---

* I wanted to show what a classical translation of Hafiz would read like. This version
has an intriguing history to me, as its source is Meher Baba's direct translation from
the original Persian. The wonderful Australian poet, Francis Brabazon, rendered this
poem somewhat, and read it out to Meher Baba, in India, in 1962, at an event called
the East-West Gathering. This poem is based on Ghazal 284 in the Wilberforce Clarke
work. I too have added slightly to the poem, as seen presented here. And I found it a
great coincidence that part of this original Hafiz poem was then made world famous,
by Khaled Hosseini in his book, *A Thousand Splendid Suns*, published in 2007.

DECEMBER 40??? *

ADIOS

Not
wanting
to seem impolite,
when the deer ran off she
raised her beautiful
white tail and
waved

goodbye.

---

* December 40th??? Why not? They had *things* like that on planet *Zicom 17*, a place of Infinite Possibilities, that was once wisely mentioned in this book. But my agent got me in a . . . *full nelson* (remember those) over the matter, and with her being about 5.5 times my size, what can I say? *Her far-reaching heft* got me to concede; thus no timely and practical insights from—Zicom. Sorry. But don't worry. I have another book planned, called *Love Kicks the Ass of Time and Space: 40 Poems of Hafiz and Rumi*. And there, there that lovely planet will be, shining in all its primal and contemporary glory, for any who dare to gaze upon her risqué self as she goes wild . . . *ransacking butts*—left and right, and up and down, and all around. Which brings me to this: Sooo, love to you. Sooo, a hug to you. Sooo, *adios* and *goodbye* to you, from Hafiz & Danny & Ralph, LLC.

DANIEL LADINSKY

T hose interested in exploring more of the life and work of Hafiz will find much information and many different approaches to the poems in the following books, which have been helpful to me:

THE DIVAN

The Divan-i-Hafiz. Translated into English prose by Lieut.-Col. H. Wilberforce Clarke. 2 vols. 1891. Reprint, New York: Samuel Weiser, 1970.

This is the literal translation I have found most helpful in my own work. (I have a "deluxe" edition of the reprint, issued in Iran.) Clarke's forty-four-page preface summarizes the life of Hafiz and gives an outline of sources.

Divan of Hafiz. English version by Paul Smith. 2 vols. Melbourne: New Humanity Books, 1986.

The contemporary Australian poet Paul Smith has written a version of all 791 poems attributed to Hafiz. He worked for many years to duplicate or simulate as closely as possible in English the rhyme scheme and meter of every one of Hafiz's poems. The result is the second volume of this set. In the first volume, a separate 256-page book, Mr. Smith has assembled what may be the most comprehensive collection of information and legends about Hafiz, his life and times and his poetry. This first volume contains an enormous Hafiz bibliography and a fascinating study of the history of Hafiz scholarship and translation in the West, including some intriguing quotes about Hafiz and his poetry by Goethe, Ralph Waldo Emerson, Edward Fitzgerald (best known for his version of the Rubaiyat of Omar Khayyam), the Sufi teacher Hazrat Inayat Khan and many others. Emerson said, "Hafiz defies you to show him or put him in a condition inopportune or ignoble. . . . He fears nothing. He sees too far; he sees throughout; such is the only man I wish to see or be."

Selected Poems

Arberry, Arthur, comp. *Fifty Poems of Hafiz*. 1953. Reprint, Richmond, Surrey, UK: Curzon Press, 1993.

This paperback anthology presents poems by fifteen translators. It contains an excellent thirty-four-page introduction and some fifty pages of scholarly notes. The poems are printed in both English and Persian.

Bell, Gertrude Lowthian, trans. *Teachings of Hafiz*. 1897. Reprint, with a preface by E. Denison Ross and introduction by Idries Shah, London: Octagon Press, 1979.

Gertrude Bell's forty-three translations of Hafiz were considered some of the best of the nineteenth century. She supplements her rhymed versions with detailed notes about individual lines and phrases. This edition also includes ninety pages of informative essays by the Sufi author Idries Shah, the Oriental scholar E. Denison Ross, and a long translator's preface by Miss Bell.

Kennedy, Maud. *The Immortal Hafiz*. North Myrtle Beach, SC: Manifestation, 1987.

This delightful small volume is a free rendering that draws heavily from a translation of Hafiz by John Payne published privately in London in 1901. John Payne was a member of the Persia Society of London, as was John M. Watkins, whose translation is cited below. Mr. Payne was also a friend of H. Wilberforce Clarke and is believed to have collaborated on Clarke's translation mentioned above.

Nakosteen, Mehdi. *The Ghazaliyyat of Haafez Of Shiraz.* Boulder, CO: Este Es Press, 1973.

Free translations from Persian to English of 124 poems. This 370-page hardbound volume by a distinguished Persian scholar, a professor at the University of Colorado, contains 37 pages of interesting introductory material and notes. The poems are printed in both English and Persian.

Watkins, John M. *Selections from the Rubaiyat and Odes of Hafiz Together with an Account of Sufi Mysticism.* 1920. Reprint, London: Stuart and Watkins, 1970.

An informative forty-page preface discusses central themes in the poetry and includes a glossary of Sufi technical terms.

The "Path of Love" and Inner Unfolding

In the past twenty years, dozens of books have been published in English about the "classical" Sufism of Hafiz's time. However, the sources I have found most helpful in understanding the spirituality of Hafiz are the contemporary works of Avatar Meher Baba. His books give the clearest presentation of spiritual principles I have ever seen. And to underline his points, he quotes Hafiz (in his own direct translations) throughout his works. Of his many writings, I would recommend the following:

Meher Baba. *Discourses.* 7th ed. Myrtle Beach, SC: Sheriar Press, 1987.

This wonderful 433-page paperback volume is a collection of dozens of short essays on issues of spiritual life. Meher Baba discusses the spiritual path, stages of love and processes of internal development. He gives a detailed review of the work of a spiritual master and the complexities of the master-disciple relationship. He also addresses what might be called "practical mysticism" as it applies to everyday life.

Meher Baba. *God Speaks: The Theme of Creation and Its Purpose.* New York: Dodd, Mead, 1955; rev. 2d ed., Walnut Creek: Sufism Reoriented, 1997.

Meher Baba's primary work on the structure and purpose of creation and the evolution, involution and perfection of consciousness. There are many charts and diagrams and a long Supplement that includes many quotes from Hafiz to illustrate different stages of the spiritual path. Since its perspective is so vast, it is not an easy book to start with, but it is rewarding to study and contemplate.

Every place where His mouth touched, 265
Every time someone on the path, 317
Every time you open your mouth, 231
Everyone is really God, 314

Fear likes a moving target, 374
Few can escape self-made traps, 26
First, the fish needs to say, 90
For me, and for the one who is One with God, 46
For your sake we are here, 263
Forgiveness is the cash you need, 354
From man's perspective in this extraordinary game, 27
From the moment of creation, 157

Gee whiz, 251
Giving thanks is dangerous, 250
Go for a walk, if it is not too dark, 363
God and I have become like two giant fat people, 237
God brought me to an emerald field and said, 324
God courts us with the beauty of this world, 77
God, disguised as a myriad things, 337
God is always there, beside the bed of the sick, 174
God is applauding our every act, 16
God listens more to women's prayers, 249
God once made love to a saint who had a hairy belly, 376
Good poetry makes the universe admit a secret, 311

Has not the Architect, Love, built your heart, 108
Have you ever felt jealous hearing someone laugh?, 325
He didn't want to think anymore, 182
He looked like he belonged in a morgue, 198
He was gallivanting about, 329

"How can I grow and reach my full height?," 183
How do I listen to others?, 44
How do those who know of God meet and part?, 333
How fascinating the idea of death can be, 345
How long will you remain content, 28
How many times a paw touched the earth today, 144
How many times do you need to hear who you are, 24
How many times have you felt like a corpse, 330

I am a hole in a flute that the Christ's breath moves through, 3
I am at a juncture now where I never have to be serious, 153
I am glad someone thinks they are real, 204
I am like a heroin addict, 352
I am wondering if someone slipped something, 158
I better sound smart once in a while, 286
I caught the happy virus again last night, 64
I had a legitimate excuse for not going, 105
I have come into this world to see this, 358
I have opened all the windows in my house, 29
I have seen You heal a hundred deep wounds, 353
I have winced at the prospect of reading a long poem, 219
I heard that in some monasteries there were human skulls, 180
I know how most minds approach me, 306
I know of beauty that no one has ever known, 147
I know the one you are looking for, 256
I know the voice of depression still calls to you, 338

Just the deep quiet, just wanting that now, 92

Know the true nature of your Beloved, 11
Knowing how she can benefit us, 228

Last night God posted on the tavern wall, 143
Leave the familiar for a while, 356
Let this page be a coat rack, 178
Like a great film or play, 276
Like a great starving beast, 161
Like a salesman who once scored at your house, 177
Like the way the valleys of the earth cup their hands, 297
Listen, listen more carefully to what is around you right now, 384
Look at the sweetness of their play, those lion cubs, 197
Look how a mirror will reflect, 304
Look how the Creator in the form of a mother, 80
Look what can grow from one shaft, 91
Looks like you are doing not so bad, 41
Love creates a synchronicity, 271

Many are more awake, with greater abilities in dreams, 190
Many times I have been asked, *What is it like to know the Truth?*, 223
More attentive than any lover or parent, 175
Most are still a leaf spinning between heaven and earth, 57
Most live in a constant state of comparison, 281
Most that is said is really like a distant echo, 245
Mount Sinai sought my counsel last night, 307
My Beloved said, "My name is not complete," 366
My heart holds within it all form, 392
My teacher once told me a story of a great saint, 95

Names have started to admit their inabilities, 70
No one but a rebel can get their mitts on God, 50
Not like a lone beautiful bird, 14
Not wanting to seem impolite, 401
Nothing can shatter this love, 370
Now is the time to know that all you do is sacred, 364
Now that all your worry has proved such an *unlucrative* business, 179
Now with illuminating spheres appearing, 209

Once a young woman said to me, 33, 226
Once I was asked, "Hafiz, why do you write poetry?," 133
Once in mid-reach I inquired of my hand, 117
Once when I was awake and lying beside my wife, 332
Once when I was fussing with my hair, 379
One of the dumbest things you can do, 188
One regret, dear world, that I am determined not to have, 37
One who weds for a dowry, 124
Our union is like this, 99
Out of a great need we are holding hands and climbing, 398
Outside everyone's house is a great force, 110

Parallel the care the dancer takes, 75
Perhaps for one minute, 274
Picture the face of your Beloved becoming your face, 86

She had a dream that told her she was going to pass, 127
She kissed the best, a dog I knew, 12
She said I could touch her all I wanted, 120
Shortly after my rooster crowed, 247
Since the Beloved is involved in everything, 20
So tender the eye's true vision, 239

When the violin can forgive the
  past, 10
When there is a lot of confusion, 23
When was the last time you felt
  complete, 69
When was the last time you wallowed
  in contentment, 149
Whenever you, God, want to be near
  me, you are, 79
Where is the door to God?, 47
Who can fully renounce a day?, 104
Who can look each day at a beautiful
  landscape, 130
Who can turn from green to gold
  without your love?, 315
Who is really living next door to
  you?, 55
Who is to say that Moses was
  not sweet on a local
  pinup girl, 203
Who laughs the most knows the
  most, 207
Who would want to leave your side,
  God, 280
Who would want to live with some
  crickets, 128
Why complain about life if you are
  looking for good fish, 145

Why just show you God's menu?, 8
Why would a rich man sweep the
  streets, 322
Wine is like the Lord Jesus, 103
Wise the beggar or the thief, 154
With them being all around my
  house, 164

You are like a wisteria vine, 82
You are newly hatched, 260
You can return to Springtime
  whenever you want, 32
You don't have to act crazy
  anymore, 362
You entered form to give a holy
  message, 284
You might think twice about leaving
  the sidelines, 58
You must have seen yourself by
  now, 248
Your destiny is winding toward the
  Perfect, 119
Your fidelity to love, that is all you
  need, 184
Your soul could have chosen a
  different kind of body, 166
Your thousand limbs rend my
  body, 167

AVAILABLE FROM PENGUIN

I Heard God Laughing
Poems of Hope and Joy

With uncanny insight, Hafiz captures the many forms and stages of love. His poetry outlines the stages of the mystic's "path of love"—a journey in which love dissolves personal boundaries and limitations to join larger processes of growth and transformation. *ISBN 978-0-14-303781-1*

The Subject Tonight Is Love
60 Wild and Sweet Poems of Hafiz

To Persians, the fourteenth-century poems of Hafiz are not classical literature from a remote past, but cherished love, wisdom, and humor from a dear and intimate friend. Perhaps, more than any other Persian poet, it is Hafiz who most fully accesses the mystical, healing dimensions of poetry. Through Ladinsky's translations, Hafiz's voice comes alive across the centuries, singing his message of love. *ISBN 978-0-14-019623-8*

Love Poems from God
Twelve Sacred Voices from the East and West

Bringing together the timeless works of twelve of the world's finest spiritual writers, six from the East and six from the West, Daniel Ladinsky once again reveals his talent for creating inspiring, profound, and playful versions of classic poems for a modern audience. *ISBN 978-0-14-219612-0*

The Gift
Poems by Hafiz, the Great Sufi Master

With this stunning collection of 250 of Hafiz's most intimate poems, Daniel Ladinsky has succeeded brilliantly in capturing the essence of one of Islam's greatest poetic and religious voices. Each line of *The Gift* imparts the wonderful qualities of this spiritual teacher: an audacious love that empowers lives, profound knowledge, wild generosity, and a sweet, playful genius unparalleled in world literature.

> *"There are universes inside Hafiz, a lineage of masters.*
> *Daniel Ladinsky follows the playfulness; the rascal moves well."*
> —COLEMAN BARKS

ISBN 978-0-14-019581-1